Your Soul Will Live Forever

Dilene Leila Swofford

Dedication

To my loving husband, Layne Swofford, and my precious son, Anders Charles Herrman— you are the heart of my journey and the light in my days.

May our souls always walk together in faith, love, and the eternal hope we have in Jesus Christ.

Acknowledgment

To God and Jesus, who have been my inspiration and guiding light throughout this writing journey. His wisdom, grace, and divine guidance inspire me to share how amazing and powerful He is. "This book is dedicated to honor and glorify his name, Jesus Christ of Nazareth, a name that has power whenever it is mentioned."

This dedication is sincere and acknowledges God's work as a source of inspiration, transformation, and guidance in my life. It reflects a deep gratitude and reverence to God for His presence and influence throughout this blessed journey of my life and the life of my family. Amen!

"To my dear husband, Layne, your infinite patience, love, and encouragement were fundamental during the process of finishing this book. I will be eternally grateful for your unwavering support and for believing in my dreams."

"To my incredible son, Anders, whom I am proud of for being a great and honorable young man, transformed into a light by God. I have seen him grow in the way of Jesus, and he has helped me, having been used by the hands of God to restore me and bring me back to the eternal, saving our home. God works in mysteries."

Sometimes, God breaks us into pieces in situations that we do not immediately understand. However, when you are willing to put everything in His hands and ask for His help, He will restore you and give you everything in double: happiness, confidence, and, above all, the ability to deal with adversity, overcome problems, and adapt to difficult situations. You will be resilient, and He will increase your faith. When you look back, you will realize that everything you went through that broke you into a thousand pieces at that moment hurt you, left you flat, was not easy, and was not what you had planned, but our Father God did everything so that you would find the right path.

He already knew the result, and everything was for your good. You did not realize it at the time. But now it is all so clear because God has taken the blindfolds off your eyes, and you see what you did not see before. Those shards, broken pieces, all come together again and become more resilient.

That is how God works: He breaks us to make us stronger and to make us grow.

We gain more trust in Him, more understanding, and the certainty that God is in control of all things. This is a necessary process of transformation and purification.

Sometimes, we ask God to help us and then complain about going through something difficult or painful. However, sometimes, it is necessary to go through difficult times in order to get to the right place that God has prepared for us.

1 Peter 1:7

These have come so that the proven genuineness of your faith—of greater worth than gold, which perishes even though refined by fire—may result in praise, glory and honor when Jesus Christ is revealed.

About the Author

Dilene Leila Swofford is a dual citizen of Brazil and the United States. Born in Londrina, Brazil, she holds a degree in computer Graphic Design and is also a licensed dispensing optician (LDO) in the state of Georgia.

She has lived between Florida and Georgia for over 25 years, staying rooted in her faith. Dilene is trilingual – fluent in Portuguese, Spanish, and English – and passionate about reaching people from all walks of life.

This is her first book, inspired by the moment in her life was completely transformed through a personal encounter with Jesus Christ.

When Jesus touches your heart, your life will never be the same!

Please be advised that this book was written from my personal point of view. It reflects what I have learned through years of Bible study, attending church, and my own spiritual journey. I understand that others may have different perspectives or interpret things differently—and that's okay.

I'm not trying to convince anyone to simply accept my words as truth. Rather, my hope is to encourage you to do your own study, seek understanding for yourself, and always test what others say—including me—against the truth of God's Word. Let the Bible be your ultimate guide.

Table of Contents

Do you know where your soul will go when you leave this temporary world, in the presence of Jesus or without His presence, forever with no possibility of return or change?

How can you save your soul, which will live forever?

Start your inner and outer transformation and get to know the mysteries of God.

Or live the pleasures of the temporary carnal world and lose your salvation. The decision is yours!

Whispers of Purpose: The Story That Chose Me

One incredible thing happened while I was working on this book.

Originally, *Your Soul Will Live Forever* was supposed to be my second book. My first book was meant to be a deeply personal testimony—sharing my life journey, the path God led me on, and how I became the person I am today. I had already written over 30 pages, gathered research, and asked family members questions. For two years, I tried to finish it, but no matter how hard I tried, I could not fully focus.

Then something unexpected happened: One simple mistake—and the entire manuscript was gone, accidentally deleted. It was a discouraging and emotional moment. But in my attempt to recover it, I began reading through old notes, prayers, and reflections—things I had written while living in the United States. As I read through them, something transformational happened. God began to stir my heart in a new way.

Instead of continuing with the book about my life, I felt led to write something else—something even more urgent. I felt God calling me to write about salvation, about the transformation of the soul and the heart, and about His truth. He did not want me to focus on my story just yet—He wanted me to focus on Him.

Each of us is unique, and God speaks to us in different ways. As we grow in our relationship with Him, we become more sensitive to the Holy Spirit, who dwells within us. For a long time, I had felt a desire to help people, but I did not know how. I tried many different things, always searching for how to do good. Still, I sensed that God had something greater in store for me.

So I began to pray, asking God to reveal the hidden gift within me—the purpose He had prepared for my life. I wanted to use it not for my own recognition, but to lead others to their purpose, to salvation, and to glorify His name.

This book is the result of that prayer. It was not part of my original plan, but it was clearly part of God's. Some days I wrote for an hour, and on other days only for a few minutes. Sometimes weeks—or even months—would pass without progress. Life was full of distractions, and I often was not fully committed. Yet through it all, I kept jotting down ideas and inspirations, believing they would eventually come together.

Nearly a year passed. Then one day, something shifted. I began thinking about the book every single day. A deep sense of urgency and conviction weighed on my heart. I had asked God to show me how to help others—and He had. And yet I had been putting it off.

That realization changed everything.

I knew this project came from God, and I could no longer delay. I gave it my full attention—writing for hours each day, determined to finish what He had asked me to begin. It was not easy. It took long hours, deep focus, and real sacrifice. But God gave me the strength, and little by little, the book came together until it was finally complete.

I have learned that starting something is easy—but finishing it takes faith, discipline, and obedience. I have also learned that when God places a calling on your life, He will hold you accountable for it. Writing about salvation was never part of my original plan. But it was God's plan—and that is what makes it so beautiful.

Only God can take an ordinary person and give them an extraordinary mission. He gives us dreams greater than anything we could imagine. And when those dreams come from Him, we must follow—because He will bless every step, from beginning to end.

To Him be all the glory.

For Whom This Book Was Written

No matter what age you are, this book will help you live a meaningful life and achieve success in everything you do. You will discover the transformative power of Jesus' name and how it can reshape any situation and transform a person from the inside out. Life will take on a greater meaning, giving you a clearer purpose. You will understand that what is impossible for man is not impossible for God. He can do anything.

I have learned that life unfolds in unexpected ways. Sometimes, we make our plans, yet some doors close while others open, redirecting our paths. Sometimes, opportunities arise that challenge our original course, leaving us uncertain about which direction to take. The Bible offers guidance and principles that can help us face such uncertain situations.

One of the most powerful steps we can take is to pray for wisdom and knowledge.

James 1:5 says:

"If any of you lacks wisdom, let him ask God, who gives generously to all without blame, and it will be given to him."

Many of us enter adult life filled with uncertainty and insecurity. Many times, we do not have a clear path to follow once we have grown up. There comes a time when we have to choose a path and follow it. Unfortunately, many lose their way or give up, and that is precisely what we must avoid: losing our balance and hope.

We all face challenges in life, regardless of our economic background or family ties. We all experience hardships at our school, in our relationships, or at work.

These hardships should never define us and our future. Their only impact on you should be on refining you and growing you into a better person. Use these struggles and challenges to understand others' pain and help them. When you prevent your pain from limiting you, and use it as a tool to build each other up, you will grow, gain wisdom, and build resilience for your future.

Every goal in life requires sacrifice and unwavering conviction. Especially in the modern day and age, everyone prioritizes acceptance among peers, society, and social groups over integrity; many people change themselves just to blend in. This pressure is leading our children and teenagers, the next generation, down a dangerous path. We see rising confusion, increasing hopelessness, and a rejection of what is good and true. Deception has become a sad way of life.

Look around you. The world is different today. What was once considered true is now contested. What was once wrong is now celebrated. There is a coordinated effort to rewrite reality. In this chaos, those who still cling to God are being increasingly isolated. However, there is something the system cannot control: the faith of those who see beyond the illusion.

The **Book of Proverbs** is one of the most powerful tools in the Bible for teaching us **how to live a righteous life** – a life that pleases God, blesses others, and leads us in the way of truth, wisdom, and eternal reward.

I strongly encourage you – **take some time and read the entire Book of Proverbs**. Do not rush through it. Read it with an open heart and a teachable spirit. You will gain **wisdom, knowledge, and understanding** – not just for your mind, but for your soul.

This book is filled with God's truth for how to live righteously, make wise choices, avoid sin, and walk in the fear of the Lord. It will **open your eyes** to things you may never have noticed before, and it will **challenge you** to examine your life and turn fully to God.

The world offers opinions, but **Proverbs gives you divine truth**.

Take it seriously. Let it correct you, shape you, and guide you. If you truly want to live for Jesus, **this is one of the best places to start**.

How Can You Save Your Soul, Which Will Live Forever?

Choosing eternal life over temporary life - this choice determines whether you will spend eternity with God in heaven, surrounded by His love, or in darkness, separated from Him forever, with no possibility of change after death.

Do not miss this opportunity today. Tomorrow is not guaranteed to anyone, so we do not know when our last day on this earth will be.

Only God can save your soul—Your soul will live forever in God's presence or be separated from Him forever.

Begin your inner and outer transformation and discover the mysteries of God.

Or follow the fleeting pleasures of this world and walk the path that leads to destruction.

The decision is yours.

Matthew 16:25-26

25   For whoever wants to save his life will lose it, and whoever loses his life for my sake will find it.

26   For what does it profit a man if he gains the whole world and loses his soul? Or what will a man give in exchange for his soul?

Do You Know Where Your Soul Goes When You Die?

This is the most important question of our lives. Do you know the answer? If not, this book was written for you, and it will help you understand what most people overlook or fail to grasp.

Worst of all, most people do not even think about it.

By reading this book, you will be able to make your own personal decisions and help others along the way.

Know that nothing can replace the Bible, and nothing ever will. In the Bible, you will find answers to all your questions and doubts. However, we must also understand that, as human beings, our understanding is limited. We may not understand every verse in the Bible, but our limited understanding does not make the book less truthful.

The salvation of you and your family is the most vital pursuit in life, for it leads to eternal life with God. No amount of money, fame, family ties, power, jewels, mansions, cars, yachts, or luxury can compare to this salvation in importance or value. In the spiritual world, it does not matter what you have or what you are in this carnal world. Everything you see around you is temporary, and when you leave this world, you will take nothing with you.

Ultimately, God is the origin of all creation, and everything will return to Him.

Everything belongs to Him. He is the owner of nations and lives. Leaders can fight to conquer each other's nations. They do not realize that the nations do not belong to them but to our God, the Creator.

Colossians 1:16 NIV

For by Him, all things were created in heaven and on earth, visible and invisible, whether thrones or rulers, whether powers or authorities; all things were created through Him and for Him.

Never forget that. Put God above all things, and he will take care of the rest. He knows all your needs even before you ask for them.

Matthew 6:8

Do not be like them, for your Father knows what you need before you ask Him.

From the Bible comes the spring of living water – the only water that can quench the thirst of the soul. Whoever drinks this water will never thirst again. As Jesus said to the Samaritan woman from the town in Samaria called Sychar.

John: 4:13-14

13   Jesus said to her, "Whoever drinks of this water will thirst again; 14 but whoever drinks of the water that I shall give him will never thirst; on the contrary, the water that I shall give him will be in him a spring welling up to eternal life."

If You Are Not Sure About The Fate Of Your Soul, It Is Best To Find Out As Soon As Possible.

There are only two eternal destinations for your soul after death.

1- With God and Jesus in Heaven

The first destination would be "in the presence" of the Lord – in Heaven, in the Paradise Jesus promised. Even now, He is preparing a home for each of us. When He calls us, either through the rapture or natural death, we can go with Him. But to be with Him, we must surrender our lives to Him. We must place everything – our hearts, hopes, and selves – on His altar. We have to accept Jesus as our Savior. Jesus is the only way.

2- Without God's presence forever in Hell

The second destination would be without God's presence – in the dark abyss of Hell, where there is no return and no second chance. This is where souls go when they reject Jesus and live only for the world.

I completely understand that nobody wants to hear this truth. It is hard to hear, and many do not want to hear about it, and many are offended by it, but there is no way around it to explain it in some easier, prettier, or less painful way. Sometimes, the truth is uncomfortable, even painful—but love speaks the truth, especially when eternity is at stake.

The most important truth is this: you choose your eternal destination.

God gives every person the freedom to decide—to accept Jesus as Lord and Savior or to walk away and face the consequences of a life without Him. God never forces anyone to follow Him. True love must come from a willing heart. That is why faith must be a choice—a choice to know God, to love Him, and to walk with Him freely and sincerely.

If you are reading this, it means there is still time.

Time to choose life.

Time to help guide your family toward salvation.

But understand this: Tomorrow is not guaranteed. No one knows when death will come, and once it does, there are no second chances. That is why we must live each day prepared, not in fear, but in faith.

God is giving you the opportunity to know Him. You have the freedom to receive His love and live in His presence forever or to reject it and live an eternity without His presence and protection.

The consequence of sin is separation from God, which ultimately leads to spiritual death.

The Bible Gives Several Examples of What Hell Is Like

Jesus clearly warned us that Hell is a real place. It is a place of torment, sorrow, and despair for the wicked. He described it as a place of darkness, where there would be weeping and gnashing of teeth.

Revelation 20:13-15

13   The sea gave up the dead who were in it, and death and Hades gave up the dead who were in them, and each was judged according to what he had done.

14   Then death and Hades were thrown into the lake of fire. The lake of fire is the second death.

15   Those whose names were not found in the Book of Life were thrown into the lake of fire.

Matthew 13:41-42

41   The Son of Man will send his angels, and they will take out of his kingdom all who sin and all who do evil.

42   They will throw them into the fiery furnace, where there will be weeping and gnashing of teeth.

Romans 3:23

For all have sinned and fallen short of the glory of God.

God is holy and perfect, and nothing imperfect can enter His presence. That is why Hell is described as a place of destruction and torment—because it represents complete and eternal separation from God, who is the source of all life, love, and light.

The good news is that God does not want anyone to go to Hell. In His great love, He sent Jesus to take our place—to pay the price for our sins through His death and resurrection.

Jesus made a way for us to be forgiven, restored, and welcomed into eternal life with Him.

Dilene Leila Swofford

The Spirit, Soul, and Body Connection

To truly understand yourself and others, you must first grasp one essential truth: most of the time, we are in conflict—not only with ourselves but also with the invisible forces around us.

In this internal battle, the flesh and spirit are in constant conflict, each vying for control over the soul. The soul, with its ability to choose, is the battleground. It must decide whether to submit to the desires of the flesh or to follow the guidance of the Holy Spirit.

This is why, as believers, we are called to "walk in the Spirit" and not gratify the desires of the flesh (Galatians 5:16). The soul must learn to align itself with the Spirit, overcoming the pull of the flesh, in order to live a life that is pleasing to God.

Spirit

The spirit is the divine aspect of a human being, which connects directly to God. It is the part of a person that enables them to have a relationship with the Creator. The spirit was created by God and that it is through the spirit that humans can experience spiritual life, worship, and communion with God. The spirit longs to do what is right and pleasing in God's eyes, drawing us toward truth, holiness, and spiritual growth. It is through the Holy Spirit that our spirit is regenerated, enabling us to live in alignment with God's will.

The Holy Spirit plays a central role in the believer's life. The Holy Spirit dwells within believers, guiding, teaching, and empowering them to live according to God's will (Romans 8:16, 1 Corinthians 6:19). In this way, God's Spirit works in harmony with the human spirit, leading individuals toward spiritual growth, transformation, and eternal life with God.

The Holy Spirit plays a vital role in guiding the human spirit and soul. The Holy Spirit first convicts the World of sin and righteousness, leading to repentance and faith in Jesus Christ. Once saved, the Holy Spirit continues to guide the spirit, influencing the soul (the mind, will, and emotions) to obey God's will. The soul, which has the ability to choose, must respond to the Holy Spirit's guidance in order to live in obedience to God. Without the Holy Spirit, it would be impossible to live in accordance with God's desires, as He is the one who empowers the believer to do so.

This interaction between the Holy Spirit, spirit, and soul is crucial to our experience of transformation and spiritual growth.

The Soul's Eternal Existence: In God's Presence or Apart from Him

The soul is the eternal, immaterial essence of a person, distinct from the physical body. All human beings possess a soul that will live forever, either in eternal communion with God or separated from Him. The soul's eternal destiny is determined by one's relationship with Jesus Christ.

The Soul is the seat of our emotions, thoughts, will, and decisions. It is the part of us that makes choices, processes experiences, and forms desires. The soul is deeply influenced by both the flesh and the spirit, and its primary role is to respond to these influences. When the soul is aligned with God's will, it seeks to live in obedience to the Holy Spirit. However, when the soul is led by the flesh, it can become consumed with selfish desires, emotions, and thoughts that lead us away from God.

Through faith in Jesus Christ as Lord and Savior, individuals receive the promise of eternal life (John 3:16). Those who accept Christ's sacrifice for sin are promised eternal life with God in Heaven, where they will experience joy, peace, and fellowship with the Creator.

On the other hand, those who reject Christ's offer of salvation face eternal separation from God, often described as spiritual death or eternal punishment (Revelation 20:15).

The soul is immortal, and its eternal fate is based on one's acceptance of Jesus Christ, who offers the gift of eternal life through His death and resurrection.

In Christianity, the immortality of the soul is a central belief, with the understanding that every soul will live forever— either in eternal communion with God or separated from Him. However, I recognize that some people have different views on this matter. Some may believe that the soul does not live forever, or that immortality is conditional based on specific beliefs or practices.

It is important to understand that people from various faith traditions, or even personal perspectives, may hold differing views on the afterlife.

For me, my belief in the eternal nature of the soul is rooted in the Christian churches I grew up in, both in Brazil and the United States. All the churches I have been a member of have consistently shared the same values and teachings regarding the immortality of the soul. This consistent message has shaped my understanding and deep conviction on the subject.

I also acknowledge that what one is taught within their faith community can significantly influence their views. Not everyone shares the same perspective on this topic, and that is okay.

That is why it is so important to do your own research and study. Reading the Bible for yourself is one of the best ways to develop a clear understanding of the subject and strengthen your own beliefs. Through personal study and prayer, you can gain deeper insight into what Scripture teaches about the soul and the afterlife.

The Carnal Body, or Flesh, Is Temporary

The flesh is often associated with sin. In the Bible, the inclination of the flesh is presented as leading to death, while the inclination of the Spirit leads to life and peace. The flesh is weak.

The body is physical, and it connects and interacts with the outside world through the five senses: sight, hearing, taste, smell, and touch. It strives to engage with the temporal, often neglecting the eternal.

The Flesh seeks comfort, pleasure, and self-gratification. It desires the things of the world, often focusing on immediate satisfaction and temporary pleasures. Driven by the senses, it is often at odds with the desires of the spirit, pulling us toward actions that are contrary to God's will.

Matthew 26:41

Watch and pray, lest you enter into temptation, the spirit is willing, but the flesh is weak.

Galatians 5:17.

For the flesh desires what is contrary to the Spirit, and the Spirit what is contrary to the flesh.

The only opportunity for a person to direct the destiny of their spirit and soul is while they are alive, by confessing Jesus Christ as their only and sufficient Savior. As Hebrews 9:27-28 reminds us: "Just as people are destined to die once, and after that to face judgment, so Christ was sacrificed once to take away the sins of everyone; and He will appear a second time, not to bear sin, but to bring salvation to those who are waiting for Him."

Accept Jesus or Reject Him?

Today, you are faced with the most important decision of your life: to accept Jesus Christ, who is the only way to salvation, or to reject Him completely. After reading this book, you will never be able to say that no one has told you about Jesus.

Accepting Jesus means acknowledging His divinity, believing in his sacrifice, and embracing a life of faith. It means surrendering your old ways, turning from your sins, following Him, and living in obedience to His word. This decision leads to salvation, peace, and eternal life with God.

Rejecting Jesus, however, is to deny His message, His divine nature, and the purpose of His death—to offer you eternal life. This choice can lead you to a life without hope of salvation and eternal life without his presence and in darkness. The world may offer comfort, distraction, or success, but it cannot save your soul. Serving the world leads to empty deception because only Jesus brings true and lasting life.

If we choose Jesus, we are promised a place with Him in Paradise, in the Holy City, the new Jerusalem. The Bible describes this place in Revelation 21, where the beauty of heaven is beyond human imagination:

Revelation 21: 1, 21

The square of the city is pure gold, like transparent glass.

Earlier in the chapter, the apostle John writes of an angel who measured the city with a golden rod:

Revelation 21:15

The one who spoke with me had a measuring rod of gold to measure the city, its gates, and its walls.

Then, he continues describing the city and its beauty.

Revelation 21:18-20

18	The wall was made of jasper, and the city of pure gold, as pure as glass.

19	And the foundations of the wall of the city were garnished with all manner of precious stones. The first foundation was jasper; the second, sapphire; the third, a chalcedony; the fourth, an emerald;

20	The fifth, sardonyx; the sixth, sardius; the seventh, chrysolite; the eighth, beryl; the ninth, a topaz; the tenth, a chrysoprasus; the eleventh, a jacinth; the twelfth, an amethyst.

With these vivid details, we begin to grasp the glory and holiness of the place prepared for those who choose Jesus.

This is not just a beautiful promise—it is your invitation. Choose Jesus. Choose life. Choose eternity with Him.

What to Do To Receive Jesus

The choice is yours. God will never force His way into your life or beg you to follow Him. He offers you Jesus as a way of salvation.

But what must you do? You must receive Him. You must repent of your sins, ask for His forgiveness, and choose to follow Him. You have to invite Him into your life and let Him change the way you live because no one can do it alone.

At the end of this book, you will find a prayer of surrender to God – a simple but powerful way to invite Him into your heart and ask Him to forgive and transform you.

God never invades your life without your permission. On the contrary, he respects you and your freedom. This is starkly opposite of what Satan does. He comes to destroy, kill, and steal. Satan is the enemy, the father of lies. He enters our lives without permission and without warning to destroy. His presence tarnishes your faith. The next thing you know, your life is upside down.

John 10:10

The thief comes only to steal and kill and destroy; I have come that they may have life and have it to the full.

Even though God would not force his way into your life, He is always near. He stands by, waiting for the moment you call out to Him. He is ready to transform your life, to bring healing, hope, and salvation. God is always faithful and willing to help and change everything in your life for the better in every way.

His plans for you are far greater than anything you have dreamt. Even now, He has protected you from dangers you were not even aware of. He cares for you every moment without forgetting, even when you are not noticing.

And know this: Jesus loves and protects even those who do not yet believe in Him because his love is unconditional and extends to all of humanity. His love is not based on whether you return it. It does not depend on reciprocation but stems from His desire to see everyone saved and living a full life.

As Jesus says in Revelation 3:20,

Behold, I stand at the door and knock: if any man hears my voice and opens the door, I will come in to him and will sup with him, and he with me.

Jesus is knocking. All you need to do is open the door to receive Him.

Faith

Even if we do not yet see the answers to our prayers, that is where faith begins to grow. Faith is trusting God in the waiting. And it strengthens as we spend time in His presence, especially through reading the Bible and meditating on His Word.

All of this is a matter of choice and priority.

Our time is one of the most precious gifts God has given us. Yet, we waste so much of our lives on insignificant and trivial things as social media and other distractions. Then, we say we do not have time for God's word and never find time to read the Bible. I say this not to condemn, but from personal experience – I wrestle with it too. And when I neglect His Word, my spirit begins to feel lacking. It calls out, reminding me that I need the spiritual food only God can provide.

Just as our physical bodies need food, our souls must be fed by the Word of God. When we do not nourish our spirit, we become weak, especially in times of trial, stress, or uncertainty.

God's Word strengthens us for battles, renewing our minds, healing our brokenness, and changing our lives. It can also protect us from sin and deception. The Word of the Lord is our spiritual bread because man shall not live by bread alone, as the word of Jesus says:

Luke 4:4

Jesus answered and said to him, "It is written, 'Man shall not live by bread alone, but by every word of God.

His Word equips us to resist temptation and overcome spiritual battles. It protects us from sin and deception. It reminds us of who we are and who God is.

Hebrews 11

1   Faith is the certainty that we will receive the things we hope for and the proof that there are things we cannot see.

2   It was by faith that people of the past obtained God's approval.

3   It is by faith that we understand that the universe was created by God's word and that what can be seen was made from what cannot be seen.

And remember the promise Jesus gave:

John 14:13-15

13   Whatever you ask in my name, I will do it so that the Father may be glorified in the Son.

14   If you ask anything in my name, I will do it.

15   If you love me, keep my commandments.

What Does It Mean to Fast And Pray?

Fasting and prayer are the most powerful ways of seeking God's guidance and strengthening the spiritual life. In the Scriptures, the two are often presented as a unified act of worship and humility.

God emphasizes fasting as an act of sacrifice that brings us closer to Him and makes us grow in faith. It helps us put aside distractions and focus our hearts on what truly matters. This spiritual discipline helps us grow in faith, resist temptations, and align our will with God's.

When we combine fasting and prayer, we break chains, set lives free, destroy sins, and transform lives – all through the name of Jesus. God does this through us. He uses us for His glory.

There are various types of fasting. Each person chooses the one that suits his/her life, depending on their health conditions, medication, etc. Below, I will give you some examples so that you can understand better.

If you have a health problem, partial fasting is much safer than total fasting or water fasting.

The key is not how long or hard the fast is, but that it is done with purpose and a surrendered heart. So, when you fast, pray, and present your request before God. Commit your fast to Him, and trust He sees your heart and hears your prayers.

Types of Fasting

1. Juice Fasting:

Consume only fruit and vegetable juices for a set period. You can fast for a half day, a full day, or longer – whatever suits you.

Consume only juices to sustain you during this time, and say prayers while working, driving, or even during simple tasks. Keep your thoughts on God.

2. Selective Fasting:

You can also fast by abstaining from specific food groups – such as meat, dairy, or sweets – for hours, days, weeks, or months.

This kind of fasting allows you to make a personal commitment or "purpose" with God as an act of discipline and spiritual focus.

3. Fasting of Your Choice:

Cutting out what you like best or what is meaningful to you for a set duration. The idea is to sacrifice something valuable to you and offer that time and focus to God.

4. Full Fast:

Water fast, commonly known as full fast, is the most intense form of fasting and should be approached with caution in the presence of health problems.

This is the most common type of fast, in which you do not eat anything but drink water. You can do it for 2 hours, 3 hours, or until lunchtime. There is no rule on the duration of a fast; you set your time.

Jesus probably practiced this fast during his 40 days in the desert before beginning His ministry (Matthew 4:1-2).

Water fasting can be practiced for longer periods than total fasting if your health allows.

The Word of God

Romans 12:2

And do not be conformed to this world, but be transformed by the renewing of your mind, that you may prove what is that good and acceptable and perfect will of God.

2 Corinthians 4:16-18

16   Therefore, we do not lose heart. And though our body wears out, yet our inward being is renewed day by day

17   For our light and momentary troubles are achieving for us an eternal glory that far outweighs them all.

18   So, we fix our eyes not on what is seen, but on what is unseen, since what is seen is temporary, but what is unseen is eternal.

God's word has the power to transform us – body, mind, and spirit. Unlike ordinary books that simply inform, the Bible has the divine ability to transform. While a regular book may give you knowledge, the Bible changes your heart, renews your mind, and aligns your life with God's will.

The Bible is not just a collection of ancient writings; it is the living Word of God, a sacred gift through which He speaks directly to us. Every verse carries divine truth, healing, wisdom, and direction. It reveals who God is, teaches us how to pray, and helps us discern His perfect will. The author of the Bible is God, and reading His sacred Word allows us to experience spiritual renewal and life-changing revelation.

Jeremiah 29:11

'For it is I who knows the plans I have for you,' says the Lord, 'plans to prosper you and not to harm you, plans to give you hope and a future.

Jesus Is Known in All Nations And Offers Us Various Opportunities To Accept Him Or Not.

Everyone who has ever existed, exists today, and will be born in the future, will have or has had the opportunity to hear about Jesus. God, in His mercy, gives us many opportunities to recognize and accept Him throughout our lives.

God does not send anyone to Hell. He wants everyone to repent, be saved, and not be condemned to Hell. The choice to go to Hell rests with the individual who rejects God's offer of salvation, which is free and for everyone.

If you have heard the name of Jesus, you have already been given the opportunity to know Him. Whether you accept Him or not, you will certainly hear of Him again because He continues to pursue your heart.

You see? Although everyone has probably been exposed to Jesus' life story, the decision to accept Him personally as your Savior is a choice that each individual must make on their own.

Do not wait until it is too late. Do not stop seeking Him and accepting Jesus into your life. He is the only way to salvation. There is no alternative.

Yes, Hell is real, but God does not want anyone to go there! That is why He has provided a way for us to be with Him in Heaven forever.

John 3:16

For God so loved the world, that he gave his only begotten Son, that whosoever believeth in him should not perish, but have everlasting life".

How Prayer Moves Mountains

Does prayer only work when the pastor or someone else prays for us?

Absolutely not. Prayer is powerful, no matter who prays, especially from a sincere heart. While it is a blessing to have pastors or faithful friends pray for us, we must never underestimate the power of our own prayer, especially when it comes to parents praying for their children.

Mothers and fathers learn that there is no more powerful prayer than that of parents interceding for their children. Of course, you can ask for prayer from the pastor or friends who are like the servants of God, but God has already given you the authority to come boldly before Him on behalf of your children.

Learn to bend your knees before God and pray, to talk to Him, to place your children on His altar, and ask for help. Pray from your heart. You do not need fancy words or a specific place. God knows who you are and what you want. Open your heart fully to Him. Pour out all your afflictions, supplications, and requests on His altar.

In Exodus 32, after God's people build a golden calf to worship, God tells Moses that He is ready to destroy them, but Moses prays on Israel's behalf, and God chooses mercy instead of anger. This moment reveals a powerful truth: God uses our prayers to bring about change, even in situations that seem hopeless.

So, make praying a part of your life. Pray for your children, your marriage, or any circumstance, situation, or person. Make a covenant with God, committing your loved ones and your lives to the Lord's altar, and ask Him to do everything that is beyond your reach and control, for we are limited here on this temporary earth.

One way to include praying in your routine is to join a prayer group with people you know. Sometimes, these groups are scarce. Take the initiative of creating prayer groups when you cannot find one among your neighbors or relatives.

For a long time, I searched for a prayer group in the United States. I could not find one —until my sister Jane, who lives in Brazil, created a WhatsApp prayer group with trusted brothers and sisters from her church.

We started praying for everyone in that group, starting with our personal problems, families, etc., and the prayer eventually expanded. When other people, like friends from outside, found out about this group, they asked us to pray for their issues. It was very powerful.

We fasted and shared Bible verses daily, and each person took turns bringing a motivating, insightful word from the Scriptures.

We witnessed God moving and acting in our lives and the lives of people connected in the group. When we studied and prepared the word to present to a person in the group, God automatically taught us, healed us, and grew our faith.

Sometimes, it is difficult to read God's word. Time poses the biggest limitation. But we can train ourselves to read a little every day. Set this goal and stick to it, even if you start with a few verses daily. It will initially seem difficult, but soon, it will become a habit that feeds your soul.

A mother's prayer moves mountains and breaks down barriers. God is faithful, and He will never abandon you or your family.

Deuteronomy 7:9-15 (ARA)

9   You shall know that the LORD is the faithful God, who keeps covenant and mercy to a thousand generations for those who love Him and do his commandments.

10   And who repays those who hate Him directly and causes them to perish; he will not be slow to repay those who hate Him, but will repay them promptly.

11   Keep therefore the commandments, and the statutes, and the judgments, which I command you this day to do.

12   And it shall come to pass, if you hear these judgments and keep them and do them, that the LORD your God will keep the covenant with you, and the mercy which he swore to your fathers;

13   And He will love you, and bless you, and multiply you, and bless your children, and the fruit of your ground, and your grain, and your wine, and your oil, and the young of your cattle, and the young of your sheep, in the land which He swore to your fathers to give you.

14   You will be blessed above all peoples; there will be no barren man or woman among you, nor among your animals.

15   The Lord will put away all sickness from you; none of the evil diseases of the Egyptians, which you know, shall be upon you, but He will put them upon all those who hate you.

Romans 12:2

Do not conform to the pattern of this world, but be transformed by the renewing of your mind, that you may prove what is that good and acceptable and perfect will of God.

The Invisible God, But Powerful Enough to Guard Us

John 20:29

Jesus said to him, "Because you have seen me, Thomas, you have believed; blessed are those who have not seen and yet have believed!

Trusting in God means having faith and placing our fears, struggles, and questions on his altar. By trusting, we can be sure that God will do better than we can.

This trust is often difficult because we do not see Him, even though we know He exists. This is normal because we are human beings, and we are not perfect. It takes time to trust God completely. The time needed to wholly and completely trust God varies from person to person. The more you get to know your Creator, how much He loves you and wants to be in your life, the more you will be moved because God is pure, just, and holy.

I know that many people do not read the Almighty God's Bible. Some do not understand the meanings of the words or are overwhelmed by their depth. Others do not have enough time. Everyone has their struggles. But remember that everything precious in life requires sacrifice and persistence. Victory never comes without effort.

Start your spiritual journey by praying to God. Ask Him to remove all obstacles, such as the veil/curtain, from your eyes that cause blindness to understanding His words. Then, use persistence as your weapon. When you start reading and do not understand, do not give up. Eventually, when God opens your eyes and mind, you will be moved, you will cry, and you will feel God speaking to you so intensely that it will change who you are forever. The journey is difficult, but the outcome is profound. It will make you open your eyes to the truth, and you will never be able to deny the existence of God and Jesus.

Sometimes, we fall into the trap of thinking that God is present in the lives of others but not in our own. It is a lie from the enemy made up to make us feel inferior, small, and forgotten.

The truth is quite the opposite. God sees you. He is incredible. He touches, changes, and speaks to each one of us in a personal and individual way. He makes Himself available to be near you as if you were the only person in the world.

It is equally important to understand that God is not an emotion but the truth. Sometimes, we feel His presence as emotion, such as a shiver. At other times, He remains too subtle to be sensed. We often think God is not near because we do not feel his presence emotionally.

But even when you do not feel anything, He is still there. He is with you at all times. God is consistent and faithful. The more time you spend in prayer and His Word, the more you sense His voice and direction.

Sadly, many people know God. They are experts in the Bible and know many verses by heart, but they do not have a personal relationship with the Father. They have been going to church for years and even serve in their work, but they have never had a personal relationship with the Father.

When you have a personal relationship with God, you will understand that He will guide you at every moment. You know that God's desires and dreams for you are much greater than your own. He knows you better than you know yourself.

Revelation 22:13

I am the Alpha and the Omega, the First and the Last, the Beginning and the End.

What Should I Do: Accept God's Truth or Follow the Doctrines of This World?

At the heart of it, the choice between accepting God's truth and the teachings of this world is ultimately a choice between eternal life and temporary comfort. God's truth, revealed through His Word, is unchanging, holy, and leads to salvation, while the teachings of this world are constantly shifting, often rooted in self-interest, pride, and deception.

Today, we live in a morally confused and misguided world. Oftentimes, people are not just confused in their actions and their paths; they are actively trying to sell their morality to the masses. Unsurprisingly, these moral values and doctrines do not come from God but have resulted from personal interests and ease. Believing themselves righteous, these people do not see the truth and want to force their worldview on the rest of the world.

Those who have studied the word of the Lord know that only God has divine knowledge, and He shares it with those who accept Him. This diving knowledge is ultimate, and the truth has set us free. It is easy to judge modern doctrines of the world through the lens of morality and ethics to know these standards are not correct. The next step is to reject these doctrines despite their widespread acceptance in society. We often feel pressured to follow these worldly trends because they are in fashion now, but we do not have to.

In the society of blind followers of amoral influences, be different and act according to the word of the Lord. Just because a practice has gained public acceptance, do not accept what is wrong as right. The world and its doctrines may change, but what is right will always be right, and what is wrong will always be wrong.

Matthew 24:35

The heavens and the earth will pass away, but my words will never pass away.

What is right in God's eyes is right—because He alone sets the standard for righteousness.

Psalm 119:137

Righteous are You, O Lord, and upright are Your judgments.

Isaiah 45:19

I, the Lord, speak the truth; I declare what is right.

The Carnal and Spiritual Worlds

God is God – eternal, almighty, King of kings, and Lord of lords. He is the creator of all things. Even if the world seems out of control, God is still in control. So, you can put your worries to rest, because He is managing everything. In fact, everything is falling into place like a jigsaw puzzle, according to His word in the Bible. Everything that is happening around the world, hurricanes, earthquakes, on a huge scale, is written in the Bible, reminding us how important it is to learn His word.

Matthew 24:3-14 (NIV)

3   And as Jesus sat on the Mount of Olives, His disciples came to Him privately and asked, "Tell us, when will these things be, and what sign will there be of your coming and of the end of the world?"

4   Jesus answered them, "Take heed that no one deceives you;

5   "For many will come in my name, saying, 'I am the Christ,' and will deceive many.

6   "And you will hear of wars and rumors of wars; look, do not be alarmed, for all these things must take place, but the end is not yet.

7   "For nation will rise against nation, and kingdom against kingdom; and there will be famines and pestilences and earthquakes in various places.

8   "But all these things are the beginning of sorrows.

9   "Then they will deliver you up to be tormented, and they will kill you; and you will be hated by all nations for my name's sake.

10   "At that time, many will be scandalized, and will betray one another, and hate one another.

11   "Many false prophets will arise and deceive many.

12   "And because iniquity multiplies, the love of many will grow cold.

13   "But he who endures to the end will be saved.

14   "And this gospel of the kingdom will be preached in all the world as a testimony to all nations, and then the end will come."

God gave us these warnings not to frighten us, but to prepare us for what will come. The more you learn, the more you will understand the spiritual war going on around us – how our spiritual enemy, Lucifer, is fighting to destroy more souls than ever before. Lucifer has lost his place in heaven with God. He was a perfect angel, wise, beautiful, handsome, resplendent and radiant. His fall occurred when he wanted to be like God and take His throne.

Hezekiah 28:14-17

14   You were the cherub, anointed to cover, and I established you; on the holy mountain of God you were, in the midst of the smoldering stones you walked.

15   You were perfect in your ways from the day you were created, until iniquity was found in you.

16   In the increase of your trade, they filled your inward parts with violence, and you sinned; therefore I cast you down, profaned from the mountain of God, and made you perish, O covering cherub, from the midst of the smoldering stones.

17   Your heart was lifted up because of your beauty, you corrupted your wisdom because of your brightness; I cast you down to the ground, I set you before kings, that they might look on you.

Isaiah 14:12-14

12   How you have fallen from heaven, O Lucifer, son of the morning! How you were cut down to the ground, you who weakened the nations!

13   And you said in your heart, "I will ascend into heaven, I will exalt my throne above the stars of God, and I will sit on the mount of the congregation on the north side.

14   I will ascend on the heights of the clouds, and I will be like the Most High."

At one time, Lucifer was a beautiful, wise, and radiant angel. But because of his pride and rebellion, God cast him out of Paradise. He did not simply fall—he was removed by God's judgment and will never be able to return.

Now, he has made it his mission to bring down as many humans with him as possible. The enemy knows that we are the family of the Lord Jesus and that God loves us very much. He knows that we have the opportunity to live in Paradise with Jesus as a family, and he will never have that opportunity again. This knowledge makes him jealous. He does not want us to achieve what he has lost because of his sin. Therefore, he tries to blind us and destroy us by attacking us in the parts of our lives where we are most fragile and sensitive, leading us to commit sins precisely where we are weak.

1 Corinthians 10:13:

"No temptation has overtaken you except what is common to mankind. And God is faithful; He will not let you be tempted beyond what you can bear. But when you are tempted, He will also provide a way out so that you can endure it.

Do you see how things work? No matter the temptation we face, God promises us an escape route. He never allows more than we can bear. We always have the option of saying yes or no to sin. It is up to us to accept the door of escape He provides or fall into the enemy's trap.

Here, we must understand that we live in a visible, fleshly world, but that there is an invisible, spiritual world. There is a great spiritual battle for our souls – a spiritual battle between good and evil.

Many people either deny its existence or avoid talking about it out of fear. I used to be the same way – I was afraid of the spiritual realm. But over time, I came to understand that there is a constant battle between the forces of darkness and the forces of God, and that battle is for our souls.

But when I gave my life to God, He opened my eyes and showed me that we should not fear the dark side of the enemy. Our Creator and Father is bigger than the enemy, and He protects us from everything that does not come from Him.

That is why it is so important for us to pray about everything, every single day. Pray. Prayer keeps us connected to God and strengthens us for the spiritual battles we face. We must recognize that we do not wrestle against flesh and blood, but against principalities, against powers, against the rulers of the darkness of this world, against spiritual wickedness in the heavenly places, as the Bible teaches in Ephesians 6:12. Today, I have a deeper understanding of the difference between good and evil, and I realize that discernment is essential in navigating the challenges of this world.

For example, think about someone in your life – from your family or your friends – who is always causing you problems, criticizing you, being mean to you, teasing you, trying to hurt you, or saying something that will hurt you. Naturally, you will get angry and hateful and would want to do something to get back at that person.

It is very important to understand that what is acting in that person and in you is a spirit – the spirit of the enemy. It is the spirit of hatred, evil, and revenge.

Do You Know How to Overcome the Carnal World?

So, how are we supposed to deal with these struggles? The righteous method is to pray to God for wisdom and discernment to solve these "spiritual" problems and to not desire revenge.

Actively ask God to take these feelings out of your heart and cleanse you with His Spirit. Then approach the meeting and dealings with this person with prayers. Whenever this person approaches you, start praying silently, asking God to protect you and for this person to leave you alone. Most importantly, pray that God transforms their heart and yours, too.

You never know what someone else is going through. They may be going through difficult times in their lives and feeling bitterness, anger, or hatred because of these difficulties. Sometimes, they may choose to project these feelings onto others. At other times, this bitterness may result from the spirit of envy overcoming them. Yes, envy is a spirit, and if you are not spiritually aware, it can use people to destroy you.

You see, our dealings and operations in the carnal world are influenced by the spirits working in the spiritual world. When we learn to deal with these spirits after acknowledging the presence of the spiritual world, our worldly problems slowly die down.

But we only become aware of it when we accept Jesus into our lives and God opens our eyes to the truth. Once we have done that, He removes the blindfold that once blinded us.

John 8:32

And you will know the truth, and the truth will set you free.

Prayer: God's Intervention

May the Lord strengthen us and show us that we depend on Him.

Almighty Lord, I come to You to ask forgiveness for my mistakes and sins. I thank You for another day of life and for the opportunity to touch someone's life and soul. Through You, may that person make a difference in the lives of others, to the honor and glory of the name above all names: "the name of the Lord Jesus Christ." Father, at this moment, we place our lives on Your altar, in Your hands.

O Holy Spirit, speak to God and tell Him that we love Him very much and that we will serve Him with all our soul. Intercede for our loved ones, especially those who desperately need divine intervention. Father, we believe that if You want it, it will happen, and nothing can stop You. Nothing is impossible for You.

Please, Lord, help us. Where we no longer see possibilities, create new opportunities. Restore life where we do not see it. We know that, without You, we are nothing, Father. We need Your help, Father.

Take care of each person reading this book. Guide them in Your way. Purify them from the inside out. Restoring all that needs to be restored. May every morning be renewed and purified in Jesus' name. Amen.

Romans 8:26

In the same way, the Spirit helps us in our weakness, because we do not know how to pray, but the Spirit Himself intercedes for us with inexpressible groans.

When Jesus ascended to heaven, He promised that He would ask God to send us a comforter: the Holy Spirit, to help us.

John 14:16-21

16   "And I will ask the Father to send you another Comforter, and He will never leave you.

17   He is the Holy Spirit, the Spirit who leads into all truth. The world cannot receive Him, because it neither seeks Him nor recognizes Him. But you can, for he lives with you and will even be in your innermost being.

18   No, I will not abandon you or leave you orphans, but I will come to you.

19   A little while longer, and I will have left the world, but I will still be with you.

20   When I come back to life, you will know that I am in my Father, and you in me, and I in you.

21   The one who keeps my commandments and obeys them is the one who loves me. And because he loves me, my Father will love him; and I will love him and reveal myself to him."

The Holy Spirit has been given to Christians as a helper. He is our constant companion and helps in times of need, comforts us in pain, and guides us in confusion.

With these prayers, we surrender everything at the altar of the Lord. Because we are limited, there are things we cannot do or solve. We must humble ourselves, seek the help of the Most High, and He will act on our behalf.

Philippians 4:6-7

6   Do not be anxious about anything, but in every situation, by prayer and petition, with thanksgiving, present your requests to God.

7   And the peace of God, which transcends all understanding, will guard your hearts and your minds in Christ Jesus.

Psalm 121:1-2

1   I lift up my eyes to the mountains—where does my help come from?

2   My help comes from the Lord, the Maker of heaven and earth.

God's Dreams are Incomparable to Human Dreams

Focus on your God, who is greater than your obstacles.

Ephesians:6-18

Pray in the Spirit in all circumstances, with all petition and humble insistence. With this in mind, watch with all perseverance in prayer for all the saints.

When we reflect on our lives, we realize that not all of our decisions have led to fulfillment and true success. Some of them may bring difficult consequences. Even when that happens, we must not despair. Everything has a solution in God.

When you ask God to help you achieve a dream or goal, He will help. So, start by praying to God for opportunities and paths, and make progress in that direction. Overcome the distractions as they arise as much as you can and let God take care of the rest.

Always remember this. God does his part, but you also have to do yours. God opens up paths, but you have to put in the effort and do what it takes to reach that goal, dream, or desire.

God helps through prayers in unexpected ways. When you pray for your dreams, God puts you in the right places, opening the needed doors and closing the ones that lead to distractions. He clears the path to your goal. All you have to do is take a step in the direction of your goal.

At times, you may find yourself on a path that does not lead you in the direction you intended. It happens. When God puts you on a path different than one you had planned, trust in His decisions. He has better plans for you. The path God has chosen for you will always lead to better results than what you intended. Keep praying and do your best, trusting God's plans.

God's dreams are incomparable and more rewarding than ours, because they build your character, bring life, and bring people closer to God.

God will Open Your Eyes. Serving the Creator or the Creation?

This divine strength comes from God.

When you put your life in God's hands, everything will change, and it will all start inside you.

God will open your eyes, and you will see everything differently. A new world will open up in front of you. God opens people's eyes so that they can see the beauty and truth of the world he has created. This can happen when people are born again spiritually or when they pray for his help.

Only He can do this.

It is a gift that God gives us when we accept Jesus with all our heart and soul. You will only understand this when you experience it. This gift is available to everyone, but not many want it or seek it.

Often, people do not want to commit themselves to Jesus because they are too busy with this passing world, investing in material things. They are seeking money, fame, a career, etc. Others have found temporary satisfaction in their lives and happiness.

Many only awaken to reality when tragedy strikes, when sickness overtakes them, and death draws near – but by then, it could be too late depending on the circumstances.

Once you die, there is no going back. After death, the opportunities to apologize, to love, or to change your lifestyle will no longer be available.

Do not wait another second to hand over your life – and the lives of your loved ones – to the Lord God, the Father of Abraham, Isaac, and Jacob.

You do not need to be perfect or change this or that before you give yourself to the Lord. You do not have to fix yourself first.

Come as you are.

Our most high, pure, and holy God leaves His altar and enters into the rottenness, darkness, and abyss that we so often find in our lives. Then, He rescues us.

This is perfect love.

He loves us and will never abandon us. We have to invite Him into our lives, and once He has entered our lives, He changes our circumstances, our hearts, the way we think, and the way we live.

The world offers us many paths, but Jesus is the only one who offers us salvation for eternity in Paradise with Him.

All other paths lead to the abyss. Many claim the energy of space, the Universe, the sun, or positive thinking brings positive energy. These paths work for some people at certain times, but in the face of divine trials, they fail to save you. So, why not follow the Creator instead of creation, which can do nothing for you when you are on the brink of death?

Testimony

I once heard a powerful testimony on a Christian program about a mother whose daughter was involved in drugs, alcohol, and partying.

At one moment, the mother realized there was no point in talking to her daughter anymore. She could send her away, but she decided against it. She needed something unique and more convincing to help her daughter. She acknowledged her limitations and cried out to God to do what she could not.

Whenever her daughter came home in that situation, she went to her room. She would kneel down, put her hands on her feet, and pray for her rescue.

She said she did this for a long time, until God touched her and changed her life. It was with great persistence that this mother fought until God granted her victory for His glory.

Later, this young woman gave a very moving testimony on Brazilian TV.

I share this story with you to remind you how God answers your prayers. Keep faith in God and never give up on your children or anyone who needs help, be it family or friends. Do not criticize them – pray for them. Ask God to do the impossible.

With God, there are no limits. He can do what is impossible for you. Never believe you are alone; keep lifting yourself and your family up in prayer.

As I said before, what may appear to be struggles of flesh, such as addiction, prostitution, and depression, are often deeply rooted in spiritual darkness. These spirits must be expelled through prayers and fasting, making room for the Spirit of God to dwell. Remember Jesus' words (Mark 9:29, MIV):

This kind can come out only by prayer and fasting.

No one can serve two masters. You must choose whom your life will serve – will it be the god of this world, the father of lies, filled with corruption, perversion, idolatry, and the love of money? Or will it be the one true God, our holy, pure, and perfect Creator, who alone can set you free?

Decisions That can Change Your Life and Your Future

Be mindful of the company you keep.

The company you have around you greatly influences who you are today and where you are heading. The influence of our company on us makes it essential for us to pray to God for righteous companions. You must seek people in your life who will encourage you to grow, to follow the Lord, and to walk in honesty and truth.

Similarly, you also have to play a part in their salvation, encouraging them to choose God in their actions and words.

The Bible says in Psalm 1:1,

Blessed is the man who does not walk in the counsel of the ungodly, nor stand in the way of sinners, nor sit in the seat of the scornful.

Our friendships matter.

Our choice of companions can either build us up or pull us down. So, to use this influence mindfully, you must handpick everyone who will be part of your life. Surrounding yourself with positive and wise people can lead to personal growth and positive results, while associating with negative or harmful people can lead to negative results.

Do not underestimate the scriptural advice to stay away from fools, because knowledge cannot be found on their lips.

You will be blessed by taking advice from those who are wise, walking with those who love God, and building relationships with people who fear God. By committing to walk with the wise, your life will only get better!

And if you get the company of righteous people, do not forget to thank God for this blessing. Reciprocate their offerings – encouragement to follow the path of God.

I thank God that, from the very beginning of my life, I have been surrounded by incredible people who have taught me to be honest and follow the path of truth.

Each of us can think of people who played a fundamental role in our lives, who have left a deep and positive impact on our hearts.

Their presence is a treasure we will carry forever.

I am eternally grateful to my friends and to God.

1 Corinthians 15:33

Do not be deceived: bad company corrupts good behavior.

Proverbs 22:24-25

24   Do not associate with those who are quick-tempered, nor walk in the company of those who are easily angered;

25   otherwise you will end up imitating their conduct and falling into a deadly trap

Proverbs 13:20

He who walks with the wise will be wise, but the companion of fools will be destroyed.

Prayer changes the deceitfulness of the human heart, renewing us from the inside out. As we are changed, we can change our circumstances and redirect the course of our lives.

If you are seeking a breakthrough, pray Psalm 91 and fast for seven days. You will see the difference God will make in your life, in the lives of your children, or anyone you pray for in any circumstance.

Remember that God created each and every one of us and that He is all-powerful. Everything is in His hands; He is in control. Trust and believe in Him. He is the only one who can do all things.

Matthew 10:28-30

28   Do not be afraid of those who kill the body but cannot kill the soul. Rather, be afraid of the one who can destroy both soul and body in hell.

29   Are not two sparrows sold for one asse? Yet not one of them falls to the ground without the consent of your Father.

30   Even the hairs on your head are all numbered.

Talk to God. Open your heart. Even if He knows everything, because He still wants to hear the details, why do we need Him.

Mark 10:51

What do you want me to do for you? Jesus asked him. The blind man said, "Rabbi, I want to see."

Here, even though Jesus knew what the blind man needed, he still asked him.

Prayer involves powerful and transforming spiritual principles. When you apply it to your life, you will discover that with God, there are no limitations. He is the Almighty and is able to answer your prayers. He is the one who will allow you to change your circumstances and your relationships, giving you self-control and changing your attitudes, your future, and the destiny of you and your family.

The invisible God created a visible universe out of nothing. He manifests His love, His order, and His power. He has dedicated Himself to blessing people, even those who turn away from Him.

God's Love Knows No Bounds.

He created the heavens and the earth.

In the beginning, the earth was empty and formless, and there was darkness over the abyss.

Colossians 1:16

Through him, God created everything in heaven and on earth, both what is seen and what is unseen.

God's entire creation, such as the sunset and sunrise, was made for all of us. We all, even those who do not believe in His existence or those who reject it, are privileged to experience God's creation. Think about it—God does not limit His blessings to the faithful but extends them to all, even to those who do not deserve it.

The beauty and wonder of the natural world are seen as a reflection of God's goodness and artistry. People all over the world can appreciate and find joy in experiencing; essentially, enjoying nature is a way of connecting with the divine creator.

Genesis 1:26-28

26   And God said, "Let us make man in our image, after our likeness; and let them have dominion over the fish of the sea, and over the birds of the air, and over the cattle, and over all the earth, and over every creeping thing that moves on the earth.

27   And God created man in His own image, in the image of God, He created them; male and female He created them.

28   And God blessed them, and God said to them, "Be fruitful and multiply, and fill the earth and subdue it, and have

dominion over the fish of the sea and over the birds of the air and over every animal that moves on the earth.

Detach Yourself from Your Circumstances and Focus on God and Jesus.

God wants you to fully trust Him and not focus on the circumstances of your life. Fix your eyes on Him and He will do what we cannot do, what is beyond our control, the invisible, the impossible.

When you meditate on God's Word, you will feel His presence, and in His presence, there is fullness of joy and eternal hope and pleasure.

When you pray, the Kingdom of God will come to earth, and you will experience a supernatural anointing that will make you an ambassador for the Kingdom of God. Always pray in Jesus' name.

The best way to increase your faith is to read the Bible.

It will transform you. It will tell you who your God is in detail, strengthening you. God's word will make you want this knowledge to spread in the world. Then, you will want everyone to know who He is and what He can do in their lives.

Before you start reading the Bible, take a moment to pray to God. Ask for wisdom and the opening of your heart. Approach His word with an open mind to understand it, so that He can guide you in life.

Psalm 119:105

Your word is a lamp to my feet, and a light to my path.

This means that, in all the circumstances of our lives, the Bible is a guiding light.

Dilene Leila Swofford

2 Corinthians 4:18

So we fix our eyes not on what is seen, but on what is unseen; for what is seen is transitory, but what is unseen is eternal.

Sometimes God Changes His Plans to Bless Us.

2 Kings 20:1-6

1   In those days, Hezekiah fell deathly ill; and Isaiah the prophet, the son of Amos, came to him and said: Thus says the LORD: Set your house in order, for you will die and not live.

2   Then he turned his face to the wall and prayed to the Lord, saying:

3   Ah, Lord! I beg You to remember that I have walked before You in truth, with a perfect heart, and have done what was good in Your sight. And Hezekiah wept exceedingly.

4   And it came to pass, when Isaiah was not yet gone out of the midst of the court, that the word of the Lord came unto him, saying,

5   Return, and say unto Hezekiah the captain of my people, 'Thus saith the Lord, the God of David thy father; I have heard thy prayer, and seen thy tears: behold, I will heal thee; the third day thou shalt go up unto the house of the Lord.

6   And I will add to thy days fifteen years, and I will deliver thee and this city out of the hand of the king of Assyria; and I will uphold this city for my sake, and for David my servant's sake.'

This remarkable account shows Hezekiah's sincere prayer and God's compassion toward him.

Who was Hezekiah in the Bible?

Hezekiah was one of the most faithful and godly kings of Judah, known for his trust in the Lord and major religious reforms. He reigned in Jerusalem for 29 years (around 715–686 BC), and his story is found in 2 Kings 18–20, 2 Chronicles 29–32, and Isaiah 36–39.

- Devoted to God: Hezekiah "did what was right in the eyes of the Lord" (2 Kings 18:3), unlike many kings before him.
- Religious Reformer: He destroyed pagan altars, cut down Asherah poles, and cleansed the temple—restoring true worship in Judah.
- Trusted God During Crisis: When the Assyrian king Sennacherib threatened Jerusalem, Hezekiah prayed and trusted God. In response, God sent an angel who struck down 185,000 Assyrian soldiers (2 Kings 19:35).
- Healing and 15 More Years: When Hezekiah became deathly ill, the prophet Isaiah told him he would die. But Hezekiah prayed, and God answered by healing him and adding 15 years to his life (2 Kings 20:1–6).
- Flawed Judgment: Later, he proudly showed his treasures to Babylonian envoys, which led to Isaiah's prophecy of future Babylonian captivity.

Hezekiah is remembered as a righteous and prayerful king whose heart was fully committed to the Lord. His reign brought revival to Judah during a spiritually dark time, and his story offers powerful lessons about prayer, repentance, and trusting in God.

Here is the proof that God hears our cry.

Our living God had already established the day of Hezekiah's birth and the day of his death. Because the Lord's love is so great, He chose to listen to Hezekiah's cries to change His mind and gave His prophet another fifteen years to live. Not only that, He also promised Hezekiah that he would be the city's support. Even the whole city was blessed by Hezekiah's prayer.

What a wonder it is to know that an infinitely powerful and great God hears us, despite our faults and sins. Out of His faithfulness and abundant grace, He changes his plans to make us happy on this passing earth. Somehow, through prayer and humility, we can touch the heart of the Most High God.

We know and believe that nothing in this world can hinder or frustrate the plans the Lord has in store for our lives, because the Lord is the "I Am".

We will face our battles with a single purpose: to pray and cry out to the Lord of Lords, our God of Israel. We cry out to the Father with one voice, with faith in the Most High, in the name of the Lord Jesus Christ.

We do not rely on our strength or power, but only the Lord can change the destiny he once set for us. We believe in the impossible, in the miracle of the Lord. Great and dear Father, thank You so much for hearing our prayers. We know that when You lay Your hands on us, healing comes and lives are set free.

Cover us with the blood of the Lamb, protect us, console us, restore happiness to our family, and unite those who are separated. We humbly serve the Lord with all our souls. May the Lord guide us in the paths of his name. May the angels of the Lord accompany and guide our family, and may we be blessed in the name above all names: King Jesus.

Psalm 91:11-13:

11   For He will command His angels concerning you, to keep you in all your ways.

12   They will uphold you in their hands, so that you will not dash your foot against a stone.

13   You shall tread upon the lion and the snake; and you shall trample upon the young lion and the dragon.

God's Power in Times of Instability.

Jeremiah 29:11-13

11   "For I know the thoughts that I think toward you," says
        the LORD, "thoughts of peace and not of evil, to give you
        the end that you hope for.

12   Then you will call on me and go and pray to me, and I will
        listen to you.

13   And you will seek me and find me, when you search for
        me with all your heart."

We do not usually think about God when everything is fine in our little world. However, when a gale suddenly comes and takes us out of our comfort zone and our day-to-day security, we become desperate and do not know what to do or think. Then, we turn to God, seeking His compassion and mercy. We lose our stability, and despair sets in.

Beware: Such desperate moments do not befall only a few of us. Without exception, we have been through this and will continue to be through this until the end of our lives.

It is all part of the human experience.

In these chaotic times, God is by your side, waiting for you to cry out and act in your life. He is ready to help you, change your destiny, and save your soul – and the souls of your family.

Revelation 3:20

Behold, I stand at the door, and knock: if any man hears my voice and opens the door, I will come in to him, and will sup with him, and he with me.

God calls every one of us. It is not enough to hear his voice; we have to open the door and give Him permission to come into our lives and help us.

We have to give Him everything we are and everything we have so He can manifest Himself and work miracles. After all, we are limited, and God is the owner and creator of all things, including life and death.

Open your heart to God to witness His glory manifesting in your life. Then, the veil that was blinding you will be removed from your eyes, allowing you to see the world around you completely differently. Inviting God into your life makes it much more valuable and meaningful. The simplest things, like a butterfly, bright colors, birds, smell, and taste, will remind you of God's loving presence in your life. Everything will become extraordinary.

Your Creator knew everything about you even before you were formed in your mother's womb. He already knew you by name. Everything around you—every fruit, flavor, fragrance, animal, mountain, and ocean—was created by Him for your delight and benefit.

Human beings can try to replicate God's creation, but they will never reach there. These copies will always fall short and will always be flawed. That is why we talk about artificial flavors, bananas created in laboratories that will never have the same taste or texture. Because God is perfect and, at the same time, meticulous. His creation is extravagant and majestic. It is in the purity and simplicity of his word that he transforms us into new creatures.

Stop for a minute, look around you, and see the details of everything near you, for example, your food. God has created an infinite diversity of foods for us to explore in infinite combinations. It is a measure of His great love and goodness that

He provides such generous pleasure in something so basic to human life. It also reminds us daily of the Creator's goodness.

Look at the pets you have at home and pause to appreciate the detail with which God created them. Think of the variety we see in animals alone. God has created all of them.

We have different tastes, and everything He has created is meant to serve a purpose and to make us happy. Take the example of dogs. They were created to serve different purposes, such as herding, hunting, guarding, or companionship – all designed to benefit humans and provide a variety of roles in our lives.

Isaiah: 49:1

"Listen to me, all you who dwell in distant lands! The LORD called me before I was born. From my mother's womb, I was called by my name.

Personal Relationship with God.

When you have a personal relationship with God and experience Him, you will never want to move away from Him again. He will become the air you breathe, strength, victory, and certainty.

He will give you a new spirit and a new heart of flesh. You will weep for having ignored His call for so long. Then, you will remember all the situations in your life where He manifested Himself, cared for you, and delivered you. You will begin to see Him working in your life – all the ways He was there for you, protecting you, guiding you, delivering you, even before you knew and accepted Him.

He will never give up on you or your family. Whether you believe it or not, nothing in this world is important. Everything passes; we are not eternal. So, what is the point of living an empty life without an eternal purpose and without God's care? What will happen to you when all this is over?

When we meet our Lord Jesus Christ, we will leave this world with hope and assurance, knowing we were never meant to stay in this world forever. We will live this life as a journey meant to take us to our eternal home in Paradise. Paradise is where we belong.

Do not think that this life is everything. We have something wonderful waiting for us in our eternal life: to live in the presence of God. There will no longer be sadness, pain, sickness, or crying in His presence. There will be peace, love, and everything beautiful and perfect. This is not a fantasy, but His promise to each one of us.

Hezekiah 36:26-28

26   I will give you a new heart and put a new spirit within
        you. I will take away your heart of stone and give you a
        heart of flesh.

27   I will put my Spirit within you and lead you to act
        according to my statutes and to obey my ordinances
        faithfully.

28   You will dwell in the land I gave to your ancestors. You
        will be my people, and I will be your God.

To Be Part of God's Family.

The family is seen as a fundamental and divinely ordained institution, essential for the well-being of individuals and society. It is a reflection of God's character.

From the beginning, God has established families, with marriage and parenthood as the basis of human society.

God loves the family and wants us to love, care for, and support each other, reflecting God's love and compassion. God placed children in families to experience His love and learn to love others. Jesus emphasized the importance of the family, teaching about the sanctity of marriage and the need for parents to bring up their children in the Lord.

Those who love and obey God become part of a spiritual family, taking on responsibilities like protection, love, and encouragement, just like a biological family.

Ask God, in the name of Jesus, to come into your life and change whatever needs to be changed. Give Him your heart and mind and leave the rest in His hands, for He does what we cannot do. He is the God of the impossible. Nothing and no one in this world is greater than Him.

Have faith. After all, everything belongs to God. We will take nothing with us; everything will return to the Creator. Just as we are born, we will also return to our Creator. Of course, as long as we choose Him as the Lord of our lives, we will be part of His family.

Romans 8:38-39

38   For I am convinced that neither death nor life, neither angels nor demons, neither the present nor the future, nor any powers,

39   neither height nor depth, nor anything else in creation will be able to separate us from the love of God that is in Christ Jesus our Lord.

Ephesians 2:19

So then you are no longer strangers and foreigners but fellow citizens with the saints and of the household of God;

God's Care.

Psalm 32:7-8 NIV

7   You are my shelter; You will preserve me from trouble and surround me with songs of deliverance.

8   I will instruct you and teach you in the way you should go; I will counsel you and care for you.

God is able to do beyond all that we ask or think (Ephesians 3:20).

Take a moment to reflect on your life. Can you see God's work in your life? In what ways has He blessed you beyond your expectations?

God provides us with material things even when we cannot meet our needs (Matthew 6.25 34). He knows our needs and provides everything we require. But His blessings go beyond fulfilling our physical needs. He also provides us with hidden things that we do not ask for or know we need, because He knows these needs.

Philippians 4:19

But my God shall supply all your needs according to his riches in glory by Christ Jesus.

He wants us to depend on Him. It is also important to remember that material possessions should not be our main goal in life. The righteous will indeed be blessed, but it is not an endorsement. If you are not honest, your prosperity from God does not testify to His approval. It only shows how God blesses everyone, no matter their righteousness. Because God makes the sun rise on the evil and the good and causes it to rain on the just and the unjust.

Colossians 3:1-2

1   Therefore, if you have been raised with Christ, seek the above things, where Christ is seated at the right hand of God.

2   Set your minds on the things that are above, not on the things that are on earth;

Matthew 4:10 ARC

Then Jesus said to him, "Go, Satan, for it is written: You shall worship the Lord your God, and Him only shall you serve.

Just as Jesus told Satan that "it is written", we also stand firm on what is WRITTEN in the word of the Most High.

God's care for each one of us is written all over the Bible.

Psalm 32:8-9

I will instruct you and teach you in the way you should go; I will counsel you and care for you…

Here, God makes one of His promises to humanity. Believe in God's promise and have faith that God is in charge of your life and He will never leave your side. He is the one who guards you as you enter and leave your home.

Matthew 10:30-31

30   Even the hairs on your head are all numbered.

31   So do not be afraid; you are worth more than many sparrows!

Romans 8:32

He who spared not even his own Son, but delivered Him up for us all, how shall He not, with Him, also freely give us all things?

Prayer: Placing Your Family and Future on the Altar of the Lord.

Lord, we thank You for another day of life, new opportunities, hope, and faith. In Your holy presence, My Lord, I come to You for the honor and glory of the name of the Lord Jesus, to place my family's life on the altar of the Lord, asking You to work wonders in our lives.

I place into Your hands all fear, insecurity, sadness, dreams, plans, desires, thoughts, my body, soul - everything I am and everything I have.

Father, I ask that You take control of all situations from this moment on. We know that when we, human beings, have tried all other options, that is when You manifest Yourself and guard us, freeing us from everything that does not come from You.

Lord, in unity, we ask that You touch our lives and bring peace to any problems causing concern in our family. Renew and restore our health so that we may enjoy many years of a healthy and happy life with our family. Touch the hearts of each family member, especially the children who are deeply loved. Calm every soul, O Father, for the honor and glory of Your name.

I love You, Heavenly Father.

Do what we cannot do. Everything belongs to You and comes from You. We know that the Lord is incredible and loves us in a way we cannot even comprehend.

May all honor and glory be given to the name of the Lord Jesus. Amen.

Trusting God in Difficult Times.

Ephesians 6:18

Pray in the Spirit in all circumstances, with all petition and humble insistence.

God alone holds all the answers, all the certainties, and the most perfect plans. That is why we must trust Him completely and never give up, not even in our thoughts. Anyone who gives up halfway through the journey does not see the grace and the miracle waiting at the end, prepared by the Lord Himself.

None of us is exempt from facing difficulties in life. Ecclesiastes 9:11 teaches us that "time and chance" happen to us all. In other words, everyone will experience adversity at some point. When we also consider the brokenness brought by sin into this world, life can often feel painful and unfair.

But the good news is that God is on our side.

Being strong is not easy; if it were, everyone would have achieved their dreams and witnessed miracles. But when we put God first and trust His plans and faithfulness, even when everything seems to indicate otherwise, we make victory a reality. True faith means trusting beyond the visible, holding on even when we do not understand, and knowing deep within that God is still working.

When we face difficulties and suffering, we must closely examine and strengthen our faith because it is the channel that opens us to receive strength from the divine, so we can persevere. To live by faith and not by sight means looking beyond the challenges before us, knowing that God loves us and is actively working to make all things work together for our good, because He is working for our good even when we cannot see it.

77

Romans 8:28

And we know that all things work together for good to them that love God, to them who are called according to his purpose.

Prayer: Promises of the Lord That Are to Come and That Will Be Fulfilled, and Bring Healing to the Body.

O Lord God, I place this person's life on the altar of the Lord, for the glory and honor of the name of Jesus. Father, we ask that everything You have begun in their life be completed soon so that we may magnify the name above all names – "Jesus Christ", our Savior, who died for each of us, giving us the opportunity for a new life and eternal salvation.

Lord, touch every area of this person's body. Bringing them healing and restoration wherever it is needed. Humbly, I ask the Lord for restored health, happiness in this heart, a renewed will to live, and a desire to seek the Lord's presence. May this person become a means of blessing in other people's lives, saving lives on earth and souls for the Lord's Kingdom.

Amen!

Jeremiah 17:14

Heal me, Lord, and I will be healed;

Save me, and I will be saved,

For You are the one I praise.

Be Strong and Trust.

Joshua 1:9

Did not I command you? Be strong and courageous! Do not be dismayed or discouraged, for the Lord your God will be with you wherever you go.

Isaiah 41:10

Do not be afraid, for I am with you; do not be dismayed, for I am your God; I will strengthen and help you and uphold you with the right hand of my righteousness.

I do not believe in coincidence or luck but in God's plan and providence.

God created each of us to make a difference in people's lives. I believe God has planned and wants us to help each other in difficult times.

I believe this is God's plan when I cry out for someone's life. In that moment, we – His children – are called to intercede for another soul, for the honor and glory of His name.

God works in ways that we do not understand. Even when we do not see the result immediately, He continues to act in the lives of people we pray for and their families. I believe He has already poured blessings and healing on them in Jesus' name. May His name be exalted forever among us and those who do not yet know Him.

We adore you, Lord Jesus. Amen!

Even when we cannot see or understand how God works in our lives, we can still trust that He is always at work, often in unseen and unexpected ways. God's plans are bigger than what our limited perspective allows us to fully comprehend. We may not understand them, but we can choose to trust Him despite this lack of understanding.

Galatians 6:1-6

1   Brethren, if you find out that someone has sinned, you, who are spiritual, should help them to get back on track. But do this in a spirit of gentleness, and be careful that you, too, are not tempted.

2   Help each other in your difficulties, and in this way, you will be obeying the law of Christ.

3   For if anyone thinks he is important when, in fact, he is not, he deceives himself.

4   Everyone must prove oneself. Then he can be proud of what he himself has done, without having to compare himself with other people.

5   For everyone must accept his own responsibility.

6   The one who is learning God's message must share all the good things with the one who is teaching him.

Prayer and Fasting: Curing Diseases.

Almighty Lord,

I come before You in this time of prayer and fasting to place this precious life into Your loving hands. You know her completely, Lord – her struggles, her pain, and the weight she carries. I ask that You stretch out Your healing hand and touch her body, soul, and spirit. Bring healing where there is illness, comfort where there is sorrow, and strength where there is weakness.

You see the heartache her suffering has brought not only to her, but also to her family, for when one member of a family suffers, the whole family shares in that burden. So I ask, Lord, that You extend Your peace and healing to every loved one affected.

We place our hope in You, O God. Let Your blessing rest upon her life. Renew her from the inside out. May every cell in her body be restored and made whole by the power of Your name. Let sickness be driven out and health return in full measure.

Come, Lord Jesus—do what we cannot do. You are the God of the impossible, and we trust in Your perfect will. We stand in the gap in prayer, believing for Your miraculous touch. Be glorified, Lord, through this healing. We praise You, we worship You, and we trust in You.

In the mighty name of Jesus,

Amen.

"With man this is impossible, but with God all things are possible." – Matthew 19:26

The Living God Who Gives Us the Opportunity to Turn to Him.

Sometimes things happen in life that shake us. Many of us, even though we know that He is the only living God, end up distancing ourselves from Him. The enemy often uses these situations to draw us away, little by little, from our most important relationship – God.

Before we know it, we have drifted so far away from the Lord that returning seems difficult. We become so involved in the outside world that we stop seeing how it does not actually lead us anywhere. This entanglement hides the depths of perdition hidden on the other side of this path, and the enemy keeps winning one battle after another using its tools like loneliness, lack, betrayal, and momentary pleasures.

That is why God warns us to stay alert and keep our eyes fixed on Him. If we begin to chase after the things of this world, they can easily take God's place in our hearts and consume the time that belongs to Him.

Luke 21:34-35

Beware lest your hearts be overcharged with licentiousness and drunkenness or with the cares of this life, and that day come upon you unexpectedly like a trap. For it will come upon all who live on the face of the earth.

But we also have hope. We know that when God calls us back, nothing will prevent our return to the arms of the Father. He will never refuse us. On the contrary, the angels in heaven celebrate every soul that repents and is saved.

Luke 15:8-10

8   Or what woman, if she has ten drachmas and loses one of them, does not light a lamp, sweep the house, and look carefully until she finds it?

9   And when she finds it, she gathers her friends and neighbors and says, 'Rejoice with me, for I have found my lost coin.

10   I tell you that, in the same way, there is joy in the presence of the angels of God over a sinner who repents."

We Do not Have Much Time: Jesus or the World?

We do not know how much time we have left. One day, God will separate those who are His, His sheep, from those who do not belong to Him, the goats. He is giving us another chance, preparing us for Jesus' return. It will be no joke for those who remain here after the rapture. Do not play with your salvation.

1 John 5:12

He who has the Son has life; he who does not have the Son of God does not have life.

Salvation is a personal journey that often takes time. God works in you and through you to bring you closer to Him.

Following Jesus is not easy. Following Jesus requires sacrifice and commitment. If you are patient and committed enough, the process pays off. Its rewards are great and eternal.

Following Jesus can lead to a deeper understanding of God's will and purpose for our lives. It leads to a sense of contentment and peace.

When we have a personal relationship with God, He strengthens us and gives us an unwavering certainty of the right path by opening our eyes to the truth. Stay strong until the end, and you will see God's glory and be in his presence forever.

Matthew: 25:31-34

31   "When the Son of Man comes in His glory with all the angels, He will sit on His throne in heavenly glory."

32   "All nations will be gathered before Him, and He will separate them as a shepherd separates the sheep from the goats."

Jesus is the way to eternity, eternal life in Paradise.

The carnal world is its opposite. It is the way of temporary pleasure that leads to hell, captivity, and death. It leads to a life without the presence of Jesus. Ask yourself, is that what you want?

It is not worth living for the world, because that would be a mistake. The world cannot save your soul—but God can. After all, He is the only way to the truth and eternal life.

Psalms 121 (Shield of Protection)

Starting the day by listening to and applying Psalm 121 to our lives is like putting on a protective covering. It reminds us that God is always by our side, protecting and comforting us, no matter what the day or life brings. It reminds us that our true guide is from God alone, who takes us through the righteous path no matter what we are going through today. The help comes only from Him, the Creator of heaven and earth and everything in them.

Every morning, as we wake up to the fresh light of a new day, God gives us the chance to start or begin again. Just as the waves of the sea wash over the sand and wipe away all the footprints that were there, leaving the sand clean for the next day, God clears the past and prepares a new path for us. Dawn does not just symbolize a new day. It also symbolizes the promise of a new alignment with God.

Psalm 121 reminds us of God's reassurance:

"You are not alone. I am with you every second of your life."

And it tells us that no matter where we are or what we are going through, God is always with us. He protects us on every step we take up or down in life. Even in the most doubtful and insecure moments, His presence never leaves.

This psalm gives us hope, strength, and a guiding light. Let us remember his presence and his unwavering care.

Psalm 121:1-2

I will lift up my eyes to the mountains, from where my help comes.

God is not a distant observer but our ever-present help. The one who made the stars, the moon, the sun, and the beauty of our world – this great God is the One who watches over us.

Remember how God guided the Israelites through the desert with Moses for 40 years? A pillar of clouds by day and a pillar of fire by night – He never left them unguided. God maintains the same promise today. Whether our problems are clear as day or hidden in the shadows of night, He will be guiding and protecting us.

We do not rely on our limited abilities, but on God's unlimited power and wisdom. This shows us that no matter how big our mountain, the God who helps us is infinitely bigger.

Psalm 121:3

He will not allow your foot to slip. The One who watches over you will not sleep.

Every day brings uncertainties and unexpected challenges. Often, these surprise trials shake our confidence. The challenge we do not see coming is precisely what confuses us and causes us insecurity, but that fear and confusion are only temporary – God's promises are eternal.

God has made a powerful promise. God will not allow our feet to slip or move.

Remember the story of Peter walking on water? When he was focused on Jesus, he managed to do the impossible: walk on water. However, as soon as he looked away from Jesus and focused on the situation, he lost his balance and began to sink. However, even though Jesus saw his doubt, He reached out and saved him. That is how Jesus is with us: no matter how much doubt, fear, and uncertainty assail us, Jesus will never give up on us. He will rescue us and save us.

God never rests when He is looking after us. He is not like us, who need to sleep and rest; God's vigilance is constant.

Imagine a guardian who never blinks, never tires, never sleeps. That is our God. He is always on the lookout, guaranteeing our safety.

God's watchful care extends beyond individuals. It embraces families, communities, nations, and generations past, present, and yet to come.

Psalm 121:4-5

4   Behold, the keeper of Israel will not slumber or sleep.

5   The Lord is your keeper; the Lord is your shadow at your right hand.

This psalm is not just about physical protection, but speaks to something much deeper: it is a promise from God to take care of our being, our essence, and our life.

This means that even when we face problems, deep down, we know who our God is and what He has promised.

Psalm 121 - Pilgrimage Song.

1   I lift up my eyes to the mountains and ask:

        Where does my help come from?

2   My help comes from the LORD,

        Who made heaven and earth?

3   He will not allow you to stumble;

        Your protector will stay alert,

4   Yes, Israel's protector will not sleep;

He is always alert!

5   The LORD is your protector;

Like a shadow, He protects you; He is at your right hand.

6   The sun will not strike Him by day;

nor the moon by night.

7   The LORD will protect you from all evil,

He will protect your life.

8   The LORD will protect your going out and your coming in,

from now on and forevermore.

Prayer: God's Faithfulness to Us.

Heavenly Father and eternal King, Creator of heaven and earth, King of kings and Lord of lords. You are the God of Abraham, Isaac, and Jacob. You are our God.

Your greatness is infinite, and Your faithfulness knows no bounds. I thank you for Your grace, Your mercy, and Your love.

Lord, I thank You for renewing Your mercy every morning, reminding me of the eternal love You have for us. I claim the promises of Psalm 121 over our family, today and every day.

I declare that we will walk with confidence, knowing You guard our steps and watch over our path.

Lord, I acknowledge that You are our ever-present help and guardian in times of difficulty. I thank You, Lord, for being our shield and buckler, watching over us day and night, protecting our entrance and exit.

Thank You for Your divine shadow as You show us what is seen and unseen.

In the name of Jesus, I rebuke every negative challenge our family faces, knowing that You are greater than all problems.

Amen.

I declare victory over our lives in the name of Jesus.

Lord, I thank You for turning all negative things into good for those who love and serve You, in the mighty name of Jesus.

I reject every plan of the enemy meant to hinder us from walking the path You have set for us.

I rebuke any spirit of fear, doubt, anxiety, or confusion that tries to take root in our hearts.

For You have not given us a spirit of fear, but the power of love and a sound mind. Father, I lift up my loved ones before You.

May we draw near to You and experience Your true love and grace. Sow Your mercy in our hearts and guide our steps.

I pray that all burdens will be lifted from our family's life.

Comfort them with Your Holy Spirit and grant them rest and peace in the Lord.

Amen, Jesus.

Genesis 50:20

You planned evil against me, but God turned it to good, so that today the lives of many may be preserved.

God Exists Alone.

We must never allow our emotions to define who God is – or is not. God exists independently of our feelings. He is constant, eternal, and unchanging.

When we learn more about who God really is and understand His nature and character, we will realize that He is always with us, regardless of the situation we are going through. He never leaves our side under any circumstances, because of His love for us. Even when we do not feel His presence or see any signs of Him, He is still holding our hand and never lets us fall. All we have to do is call out to Him with all our heart.

As children of God, we are called to be strong – to let our faith guide us, not our emotions. If we learn to do this, we will be in control of our emotions and feelings.

Every day we wake up and open our eyes, already experiencing some kind of emotion, depending on the situation we are in. With life come joy, sorrow, peace, and anxiety.

At times, these emotions feel overwhelming, but only God can give us control over our emotions/feelings. When we ask Him to help us learn to control them, He teaches us to surrender our feelings to faith and to live from that place.

Isaiah 45:5-6 says:

"I, and I alone, am the LORD; there is no other God".

Fear and Faith Cannot Occupy the Same Space. One Paralyzes the Other.

Faith holds the upper hand over fear.

Often, we let fear, negative emotions, and bad thoughts take control, leading to despair, insecurity, and doubt. When we give way to these emotions, we open the door to the enemy's work by giving Him access to our lives.

If we learn to use our faith in all situations, especially in times of tribulation that seem beyond our control, we will experience the peace that comes from God. This means we act from the spirit and not from the flesh. Then, our faith will overcome fear and the flesh, giving us the peace that comes from God. Thus, we will have the confidence that God holds us in His hands. Peace will overtake us, even in the midst of tribulation. Only with God is this possible, because He will never abandon us. He will save our home, each and every one of us.

Acts 16:31-34

31   They answered, "Believe in the Lord Jesus, and you and your household will be saved.

32   Then they preached the word of God to him and to all his household.

33   At that time of night, the jailer washed his wounds, then he and all his household were baptized.

34   Then he took them to his house, served them a meal, and, with all his family, rejoiced greatly that they had believed in God.

Philippians 4:4

Do not be anxious about anything, but in everything, by prayer and supplication, with thanksgiving, present your requests to God. And the peace of God, which surpasses all understanding, will guard your hearts and your minds in Christ Jesus.

When we allow our emotions to control our lives, it will be chaotic. But if we learn to put our faith above all else and let it guide us, we will have more control over situations and be able to help someone who needs our help. Life will be much more peaceful.

Feelings and emotions are part of what makes us human and enrich our lives when used correctly, but they should not dictate our actions. If we let emotions lead, we allow what is visible in the world to control us, rather than the Spirit who lives within us.

God does not answer us according to our emotions or feelings, but according to His word. He has already proven that He honors His word.

God's divine intervention will be activated by our faith and never by our emotions.

Remember what Jesus said in John 11:40

Then Jesus said, "Did not I tell you that if you believe, you will see the glory of God?"

Of course, it is not easy to feel happy all the time, especially when you are going through tribulations. However, we must remember that these moments are here to teach us ways to God. To align with these teachings, we must respond with faith.

Make a habit of using your faith as your guide, not your emotions. Focus on God and not on the problem, because God is bigger than any problem. Oftentimes, God allows trials to refine us, to mold us into better, more humble people, or to change something in us that is necessary, thus making us more dependent on Him.

He wants us to believe that we can control our emotions with His help. Through His words and His Spirit, He teaches us maturity and growth in faith.

Jesus understands everything we go through in life because He lived here like us. He cried, suffered, felt fear, hunger, pain, and deep humiliation as if He were the worst human being on earth. Though sinless, He was treated worse than a criminal, spat in the face, humiliated, His beard ripped out, and whipped to death. Worst of all, He was mistreated and killed by the very people He created. Yet, through all this, He lived by faith, knowing He would return to the arms of the Father.

He suffered for me, for you, for all those who have died, and for all those who will be born. He gave Himself as a living sacrifice so that all of us would have the option and the opportunity to attain eternal life.

Isaiah 50:6

> I offered my back
>
> to those who beat me,
>
> my face to those
>
> who plucked out my beard;
>
> I did not hide my face from mockery
>
> and spitting.

> Our salvation comes through faith, not emotions.

God never said in the Bible that we have to understand everything that happens in our lives or in the world. But He did tell us that, even when we do not understand, we must have faith and trust in Him.

Sometimes we try to hide our feelings, but they remain stored somewhere in the back of our minds. It only takes one thought to affect and shake our faith.

Depending on the situation, such as health problems, family struggles, or major decisions, it may seem like nothing we do can bring change or improvement. It can feel like we have reached the end of the tunnel. That is when fear, insecurity, and questions arise: Does God see what is happening in my life? Does He know the pain in my soul?

Our emotions are triggered the moment we face positive or negative situations. That is why the apostle Paul gave us this instruction:

2 Corinthians 5:7

For we live by faith, not by what we see.

When everything is going well, when life is progressing as we want, it is easy to say how wonderful God is, that He is walking with us and blessing us. That gives us confidence and security.

But when the situation is the opposite, we feel terrible. Panic, sadness, and a sense of loss creep in. We begin to think God is far from us and unaware of our pain. In such times, depression and anguish may overwhelm us. Many give up on their faith in these moments because emotions begin to dominate, overpowering spiritual truth. The carnal side starts to rule over faith.

Hebrews 11:1–3

1   Now faith is the foundation of what we hope for and the proof of what we do not see.

2   For by it the elders received a good testimony.

3   By faith we understand that the universe was created by the word of God, so that what is seen was not made out of what is visible.

How Do You Deal with Secrets You are Ashamed of (Hidden Skeletons)?

Each of us has a few skeletons hidden in the closet—parts of our lives we do not want to face. These are the dark corners of our past or present, places where sin has taken root. They are signs of temptations of the flesh, born out of the enemy's influence. Avoiding these skeletons may seem convenient, but doing so only strengthens them.

Some may have fewer than others, but everyone carries these hidden burdens, even if they deny their presence. Some of these secrets involve sinful desires or covert addictions. Others take the form of behaviors that people feel too powerless to resist. Many hide their wrongdoing—lust, dishonesty, envy, pornography, foul language, alcohol abuse, or secret relationships—behind a mask. Some sins may appear greater, others lesser, but all weigh on the soul when left unaddressed.

Sooner or later, we must confront them. If we do not, these hidden struggles may one day be exposed. When that happens, the world will see who we truly are when no one is watching.

These are often secrets known only to ourselves—and to God. Nothing is hidden from Him; nothing escapes His sight. He knows your heart and your thoughts. He knows that even when our conscience tells us something is wrong, the craving for momentary pleasure can override our better judgment. We may feel gratification for a moment, but afterward, the soul mourns. Sin distances us from God.

Yet we have hope in God and in His mercy. Repentance is not easy—if it were, no one would hide these skeletons. We cannot overcome sin by our own strength. We need divine help. We must surrender everything to God, asking Him to purify our minds, renew our souls, and give us clean hearts. Only by inviting Him into our weakness can we find strength and freedom.

God will destroy the chains that bind us and purify our hearts—if we come to Him with genuine repentance and a true desire to change.

But we must also guard our hearts and remain vigilant, so we do not return to the same sins, like a dog returning to its vomit (Proverbs 26:11). We are called to be firm in our resolve, and we are promised that such steadfastness will bring eternal reward.

The Bible is clear: sinners will not inherit the Kingdom of God.

Revelation 21:27

"Nothing impure will ever enter [heaven]"

At the same time, the same Bible declares the mercy of God—that all sinners can be forgiven when they turn to Him.

Revelation 22:14-15 (NIV)

14   Blessed are those who wash their robes, that they may have the right to the tree of life and may go through the gates into the city.

15   Outside are the dogs, those who practice magic arts, the sexually immoral, the murderers, the idolaters, and everyone who loves and practices falsehood.

Mental and Spiritual Battle

Have you ever heard of the mental and spiritual battle? Whether or not we realize it, every one of us goes through it on a daily basis. It is a deep, invisible struggle that we fight not only in our minds but also in our souls. We live in a spiritual world where many significant things are hidden from our eyes—this battle being one of them. It is a war between God's angels and Satan's fallen ones.

The enemy knows how deeply God loves His creation and how much He desires to save us from the deception of this world. That is exactly why Satan seeks to hurt God by targeting His creation—by hurting us through lies, deceit, and destruction.

Jesus Himself said in John 14:30:

"I will not say much more to you, for the prince of this world is coming. He has no hold over me."

Yes, Jesus called Satan the prince of this world. He warned us that Satan holds a measure of influence over this fallen world. And our beloved Savior also warned that this prince will use his power against humanity: to steal, kill, and destroy (John 10:10).

Drugs, perversion, alcohol abuse, and excessive attachment to worldly pleasures—without regard for our well-being or boundaries—are just a few of the tools the enemy uses to entrap us.

Many people believe that this life is all there is, that once we die, it is over, but that is not true. The enemy offers power, pleasure, and false security to lure people into following him.

Some enter this deal knowingly, choosing the temporary over the eternal. Others simply do not believe in the existence of life with Jesus. Regardless of the reason, they will have to pay the price. And unless they repent and turn back to God, that price will be their very soul.

But there is hope—God loves you. He wants to rescue you. He wants you to live with Him forever. The choice is yours: invite Him into your life or keep Him out.

Satan will do anything to keep you from seeing the truth. He knows he can never return to Heaven or be with God again, so his mission is to drag as many souls away from God as he can.

The enemy is not like God—he does not honor your free will. He just needs a loophole, a small opening, to enter your life. In today's world, those openings are everywhere. With a single click, temptation is in the palm of your hand. What was once clearly wrong is now widely accepted. What used to be taboo is now celebrated. The world has blurred the lines, and the enemy rejoices when we forget where truth ends and deception begins.

Yet in the midst of all this, God still speaks. He still fights for your soul. He keeps showing us that the broad road of sin and carnal pleasure leads away from Him and straight to hell. But He also points us toward the narrow road—the path that leads to life. He continues to reveal the righteous way, day after day.

You may have heard of Jesus before. You may know that He said:

"I am the way, the truth, and the life. No one comes to the Father except through me" (John 14:6).

If you have heard that, ask yourself: What have I done with that truth?

Your life and your time are not guaranteed. None of us knows how many days we have left on this passing earth.

These are the words of God.

As Psalm 39:5 says:

"You have made my days a mere handbreadth; the span of my years is as nothing before you. Everyone is but a breath, even those who seem secure."

Psalm 144:4 echoes this:

"Man is like a breath; his days are like a fleeting shadow."

And James 4:14 reminds us:

"You do not even know what will happen tomorrow. What is your life? You are a mist that appears for a little while and then vanishes."

The truth is, we do not know what the future holds. Tomorrow belongs to God, and He governs all time. Our lives depend on Him, and all our plans must submit to His will.

Today is the day of decision. Choose truth. Choose life. Choose Jesus.

What Should We Prioritize in Our Lives?

In today's world, we have more convenience than ever before, all designed to save time. And yet, we find ourselves constantly running, busy from morning till night, moving from one thing to the next... and still feeling like we have gotten nowhere.

Have you ever stopped to ask: Where is my time with God?

Know that spending some time praying to God and serving His path is very important. We must take time to build our relationship with our Creator and not spend every waking minute chasing worldly pleasures. Still, are we getting this time? Or are we too preoccupied with the distractions created by our personal lives, business, and family that we are left with no breathing moment?

Everything that we work for—from our bodies to families and businesses—will be left behind. We will not gain its benefits in our lives with Jesus. In that life, only the time we spent building our relationship with God will make us happy.

But we are waiting for the next day to start spending that meaningful time. While waiting, we often forget the two things that can happen suddenly, robbing us of the opportunity to build this relationship. These things are death and rapture.

Death will come suddenly, leaving us with no time to mend our ways.

Or the rapture will happen, and we will only rejoice in it if we have already proven ourselves to be in Jesus' presence in eternal life.

We have to stay prepared for either of these, so we can rejoice in the presence of our Savior when the time comes.

Matthew 24:36-39

36   As for the day and the hour, no one knows, neither the angels of heaven, nor the Son, but only the Father.

37   As it was in the days of Noah, so it will be at the coming of the Son of Man.

38   For in the days before the Flood, the people were eating and drinking, marrying and giving in marriage, until the day Noah entered the ark;

39   and they knew nothing until the Flood came and took them all away. So it will be at the coming of the Son of Man.

We learn from these verses that we must keep assessing ourselves to answer: Are we ready to meet Jesus?

Do not wait. Tomorrow is not promised.

The time to turn to God is now.

If Jesus Returns Today, Are You Prepared? What If It is Your Last Day on Earth?

When you give your life to Jesus, you are promised eternal salvation. The moment your eyes close in this world, they will open in His presence. You will be embraced by the One who gave His life for you, so that you could live forever with Him in perfect peace.

Romans 10:13

"For everyone who calls on the name of the Lord will be saved."

John 3:16

"For God so loved the world that He gave His one and only Son, that whoever believes in Him shall not perish but have eternal life."

This is the promise of God. If you walk with Jesus, there is no reason to fear His return. In fact, you will prepare for it. It is not so much about when or how He will return, but how well you are living the time He has given you. Are you using it to grow closer to Him?

The apostle Paul asks us to reflect deeply:

Is there anything you would regret not doing if your time on earth ended today?

Is there someone you need to forgive?

Is there a sin you need to leave behind?

What about the calling from God you have been postponing?

Fulfill your duties before it is too late.

The time to act is now.

1 Thessalonians 5:15

"Make sure that nobody pays back wrong for wrong, but always be kind to one another and to everyone."

Life on earth is short, fleeting like a breath. One moment we are young, and the next we are looking in the mirror, wondering where the years have gone. One truth remains through joy and pain, falls and recoveries: death comes to all, and no one knows who is next. It is as if we are all standing in a line, waiting for our name to be called—only God knows when.

So the question remains:

Are you ready?

Invest in Your Salvation

While God values hard work and wants us to be diligent in all we do and achieve success, He also reminds us that nothing should come before Him. Success, wealth, and achievement are not wrong, but they must never replace God's place in our lives. Jesus said it clearly:

"Seek first the kingdom of God and His righteousness, and all these things will be added to you."

—Matthew 6:33

In other words, we must build our entire lives—our goals and dreams—on the foundation of honoring and obeying God.

2 Thessalonians 3:10

"For even when we were with you, we gave you this rule: 'The one who is unwilling to work shall not eat.'"

God wants us to be responsible and hardworking. But He also wants us to remember that everything in this world is temporary. The only eternal investment you can make is in your salvation. The houses, cars, promotions, and wealth will all pass away one day. Your soul will not.

Matthew 16:26

"What good will it be for someone to gain the whole world, yet forfeit their soul? Or what can anyone give in exchange for their soul?"

It is in human nature to yearn for meaning because we were created with a purpose firmly wired within us. This search for meaning keeps us striving, even when we do not fully know what we are looking for.

Many chase after the wrong things, believing success or pleasure will satisfy the ache. But true fulfillment comes only when we realize that God is the source of everything we are seeking. When we understand that this deep longing comes from Him—that He exists, and that His word can fill us—that is when we begin to truly seek Him.

If we prioritize God's word, our spiritual well-being and personal growth will be nourished through practices like mindfulness, reflection on Scripture, and a deepening connection with Him. This leads us to a fuller and more meaningful life.

Our quest for meaning in life is deeply tied to how nourished our souls are. So, take time to nourish your soul and seek God.

Matthew 11:28-30

28   Come to me, all you who are weary and burdened, and I will give you rest.

29   Take my yoke upon you and learn from me, for I am gentle and humble in heart, and you will find rest for your souls.

30   For my yoke is easy and my burden is light.

When Time Ends, Eternity Begins.

Many people spend their lives preparing for success, comfort, or security, but forget to prepare for what is absolutely certain: death. When I say "death," I do not mean just the end of life in this carnal world. I mean the preparation of the soul, because, after all, who can guarantee that the day will not come?

This subject is uncomfortable, but we cannot avoid death by avoiding the conversation about it. While our departure from this world is inevitable, why do we invest so much of our attention in worldly success and so little in the life we will live in the presence of Jesus? Surely, the soul should take precedence in whatever we invest in, because it will live forever. If it will outlive our fleshly body, should not we invest more in it than in material success?

Though it may seem unreasonable to some, the real reason we neglect our eternal life is that we are too caught up in this physical, carnal world. This distraction blinds us and keeps us from pursuing salvation, ultimately leading to eternal punishment.

But against this punishment, God offers a promise: eternal life to all who believe in Him. He assures us that death is not the end. Death and eternal punishment exist because of sin, but God made a way for us to live forever with Him. He sent Jesus to suffer the punishment in our place. He promises eternal life to everyone who accepts Jesus as their Savior and follows Him.

1 John 5:11-13

And this is the testimony: God has given us eternal life, and this life is in His Son. Whoever has the Son has life; whoever does not have the Son of God does not have life. I have written these things to you who believe in the name of the Son of God, so that you may know that you have eternal life.

Your salvation is possible through faith in Jesus Christ. The doctrine of Christ teaches that salvation is received by grace, mercy, and the merits of Jesus Christ, not by our own deeds.

Romans 6:23

For the wages of sin is death, but the gift of God is eternal life in Christ Jesus our Lord.

Our eternal future is secured—not by our works, but by His grace.

Your Prayer Has Power.

Know this: your prayer holds power. Every second spent in God's presence strengthens the certainty that He is with us. We build our relationship with God through prayer, fasting, and simply talking to Him. Even when we do not see His hand moving, we can be confident that He is always at work. He does not stop. He fulfills His plans at the right time—because He knows what is best and when it is best for us.

Believe in Him. Lay everything on His altar. Trust Him even when it is hard, even when hope feels far away. Ask Him to strengthen your faith, to comfort your soul, and to breathe life into your weary heart.

And every time sadness, insecurity, or despair grips your heart, pray even more. Do not give up. Do not stop praying.

Say from your heart:

"Lord, please help me in this situation. Help me to trust You. Do what is impossible for man. Open a door where there is none."

Every prayer, every tear, every whisper of faith—it all counts.

Psalm 20:7–8

Some trust in chariots and some in horses, but we trust in the name of the Lord our God.

They are brought to their knees and fall, but we rise up and stand firm.

Proverbs 3:5–7

Trust in the Lord with all your heart and lean not on your own understanding;

In all your ways submit to Him, and He will make your paths straight.

Do not be wise in your own eyes; fear the Lord and shun evil.

Let your trust be in Him, not in circumstances, not in your own understanding. God is faithful. He will make a way. Keep praying. Keep walking. Keep trusting. He is with you.

Past and Present Feelings, and Forgiveness

God's forgiveness consists of forgiving sins and restoring communion with Him. Forgiveness is a gift of mercy and grace that can be received through repentance and faith.

Divine forgiveness requires repentance and faith in Jesus Christ. In addition, we are also called to forgive those who have offended us.

1 John 1:9

If we confess our sins, He is faithful and just to forgive us our sins and to cleanse us from all unrighteousness.

Matthew 18:21-22

Then Peter came to Jesus and asked, "Lord, how many times shall I forgive my brother when he sins against me? Up to seven times?"

Jesus answered, "I tell you, not seven times, but seventy times seven."

Mark 11:25-26

25   And when you stand praying, if you have anything against anyone, forgive him, so that your heavenly Father may also forgive your sins.

26   But if you do not forgive, neither will your Father in heaven forgive your sins.

Isaiah 43:25

"I, even I, am He who blots out your transgressions for My own sake, and your sins I do not remember."

Romans 8:1

There is no condemnation for those who are in Christ Jesus.

Divine forgiveness has a transforming and liberating effect. God offers us a new opportunity, regardless of the seriousness of our sins or failings.

To receive it, we must recognize our mistakes and ask for forgiveness. It requires a humble and penitent heart.

Divine forgiveness means that we no longer need to carry the weight of guilt. It frees us from the slavery of sin and allows us to live a new life.

1 John 4:20-21

20   If anyone says, "I love God," but hates his brother, he is a liar. For whoever does not love his brother whom he has seen, cannot love God whom he has not seen.

21   And this commandment we have from Him: that whoever loves God must also love his brother.

If you have any feelings from your past or present, it is very important to resolve them—or better yet, to forgive. If someone has hurt you or said something painful, even if years have passed and it no longer affects you, but you have never forgotten it, then it is time to act and forgive.

Forgive that person and, if possible, ask for their forgiveness. The best way to speak to them is to tell the truth. Tell them they have hurt you with their words or actions, but you have forgiven them. They may feel offended, but that does not matter. What matters is that you forgive and ask for forgiveness if you caused them any sorrow or distress.

Forgiveness takes away an immense weight in any circumstance, and that burden will never dominate you again. Do not let your own feelings or past mistakes enslave you. We must relieve our souls, and our lives will become more peaceful and less tense. You will feel pleasure deep inside for forgiving and asking for it —it is a beautiful thing. Be humble at heart. Not everyone is able to do this because pride, arrogance, vanity, and presumption hold them back.

Also, remember that everything you have been through in your past has shaped who you are today. You have grown and learned, and you now walk at a much higher level in understanding. God has opened doors that no man could have opened, and you can see the truth: God's hand has been at work in your life all along.

It is very important not to let your past define your future or your identity. With God, there are no limits.

There comes a time in life when we want to do everything right, especially when we begin a personal relationship with Jesus, who never gives up on us. When God removes the blindfold from our eyes and shows the wonders of our Creator, then everything we think and do is aimed at glorifying Him.

The saddest thing is that many people still wear that blindfold. They do not see that Jesus exists—that He is real and alive among us. He sees and knows everything. They do not believe in Jesus or God because they have been blinded by the enemy, and only God can help them. But many are not interested, preferring to follow what the world offers because it seems easier and more pleasurable.

But that is where the danger lies—because they cling to what is false, temporary, and deceptive. Pray for these people. If you know them, tell them about Jesus.

One Breath Away from Forever.

Observe where we are today. Just look around, and you will see the signs of the last days unfolding before your eyes. Jesus is coming back—He is closer than you can imagine. Do not wait until it is too late. Tell others about Jesus so they, too, may have the chance of salvation. Do something that can make a difference in someone's life.

Do not live just to live; make every effort to help others receive God's gift of salvation, because in the end, what matters most is your salvation. Everything in this world will be left behind, without exception. Everything belongs to God and will return to Him. All things are His, for He is the Creator of everything. Amen, Lord.

If you cannot remember anything you have read in this book, remember this sentence, because it is what matters at the end of it all:

"Above all, your salvation is what matters most. Receive it, and one day you will dwell with God."

I thank God that He did not take me before I came to know Him and surrendered my life, my family, and received His salvation. There is still time—but it is short. Make the most of every moment while you can. Surrender everything into the Lord's hands, and He will take care of the rest.

We all feel that something is happening in the world. It feels like something big is about to occur at any moment, but no one can explain or predict exactly what it is or when it will happen.

Know that Jesus' return is near, and you and your family must be prepared. Believe me, you do not want to be left behind after the rapture. There will be seven years of great tribulation, during which the world will face the most intense anguish in living memory. If you think today is terrible, imagine what it will be like then. Today is just the beginning of labor pains.

1 Thessalonians 5:1–6

1   Now, brothers and sisters, we do not need to write to you about times and dates,

2   for you know very well that the day of the Lord will come like a thief in the night.

3   While people are saying, "Peace and safety," destruction will come on them suddenly, as labor pains on a pregnant woman, and they will not escape.

4   But you, brothers and sisters, are not in darkness so that this day should surprise you like a thief.

5   You are all children of the light and children of the day. We do not belong to the night or to the darkness.

6   So then, let us not be like others, who are asleep, but let us be awake and sober.

Being prepared for the Second Coming of Jesus Christ means building a close relationship with Him through prayer and the reading of God's Word.

Jesus is the only way to salvation and hope. Once you give your life to Him, your spiritual eyes will be opened, and you will see the truth. Then, this truth will set you free. Invite Jesus into your life. Talk to Him, and you will come to know that He will do everything for you. Your life will never be the same again—He will transform you.

One way to build an intimate bond with the Lord is by reading the Bible. The more you read the Bible—His Word—the more your faith will grow, and you will be transformed and restored. You will become a new creation.

We are certainly heading toward the end, and the return of Jesus Christ is closer than we can imagine.

Many remain blind, even as they witness calamities all around. Others feel anxious because of the events unfolding around us. But we must not lose hope. Even if everything seems chaotic, know that Jesus is still on the throne, and everything remains under His control and dominion. He is our Creator.

There is a song I really love in English, and it goes like this:

Sometimes I fall to my knees and pray

Come, Jesus, come, let today be the day

Sometimes I feel like I am gonna break

But I am holding on to a hope that would not fade

Stand Firm in Your God.

Isaiah 50:10

Who is there among you who fears the Lord and listens to the voice of His servant? When you are in darkness, without any light, trust in the name of the Lord and stand firm in your God.

Sometimes, even those with great responsibility go through moments of deep darkness. Maybe today, you are going through a season when you feel overwhelmed by sadness, fear, or the sense that you have no strength left to continue. We all come to this chapter in life at some point. I believe that many of the most important lessons in life are learned in the midst of tribulation, because that is where we grow. Similarly, there are treasures we can draw from Elijah's story and from this verse.

Do you know the story of Elijah? He was a prophet of Israel in the 9th century BC, known for his courage and faith in the God of Israel. Elijah confronted the idolatry and social injustices of King Ahab.

1 Kings 19:1-4

1   When Ahab told Queen Jezebel what Elijah had done—that he had killed all the prophets of Baal—

2   she sent word to Elijah: "You have killed my prophets, but I swear to you by the gods that this time tomorrow, I will kill you."

3   Elijah decided to flee in order to escape alive. He went to Beersheba, a town in Judah, and left his servant there.

4   He continued alone through the desert, walking all day. At one point, he sat down under a juniper tree and prayed for death to take him: "It is enough, LORD! Take my life

now. I must die one day, like all those who have gone before me and died for serving you. So let it be now."

Look at how Elijah prayed, asking to die, weary and feeling as though life had lost its value. Imagine talking to God like that. But understand this: you do not need to pray with perfect or poetic words. God wants sincere prayer—from the heart, with real feelings and honest words.

What is most striking is that even when Elijah prayed for death, he still prayed. That is the key—he never stopped talking to God, because he knew God never stops listening. Just because God does not always answer exactly as we want or expect does not mean He is not listening.

When Elijah prayed, his words were not polished—they were raw and full of pain. Yet God was not angry or offended. He did not reject Elijah. Instead, God listened with compassion. He did not humiliate him. God simply wants us to come to Him truthfully and wholeheartedly.

"Talk to Me," says the Lord. "Place on My altar everything that is broken—your shattered heart, your sadness, your fear. I want to hear you and help you."

God already knows what we are going to ask before we pray. But He longs for us to come and pour out our hearts to Him as our Abba Father. He wants us to release the burdens we carry and find peace in His presence.

Elijah, this powerful man of God, prayed for death—yet incredibly, he never saw death. According to Scripture, God took him to heaven. Death was never part of Elijah's future or God's plan for him. Even in his darkest moment, Elijah did not let emotions override his faith. He kept praying.

His emotions told him to give up. But his faith told him to keep going. Emotions can lead us to quit just before the breakthrough, right before the victory we have waited so long for.

2 Kings 2:11

And it came to pass, as they went on and talked, behold, a chariot of fire with horses of fire separated them one from another: and Elijah went up into heaven in a whirlwind.

According to the Bible, Elijah did not die. He was taken to heaven in a chariot of fire, without passing through death.

The Foundation of Our Family: Values That Shaped Us

In the end, the most important things in our lives are the Creator, salvation through His Son Jesus, and our families.

When we are younger, we often get angry with our parents and siblings, but when we leave home and start our own lives, with our own families and responsibilities, everything changes— including the way we see them. Our perspective shifts, and we begin to value and admire them more deeply.

When we become parents ourselves, God opens our eyes to see how much care and sacrifice our parents gave us. Only then do we truly appreciate all they did—the daily care, preparing us for school, the food, the advice we once hated, and the meals our mother made that we did not want to eat. These become some of the most cherished memories once we are living alone, cooking for ourselves, and raising our own children.

Have you ever heard the saying, "You can only understand what someone is going through when you have been through it yourself?" It is true. We often do not value something until we feel its absence.

Family is precious—the most valuable treasure in life. It is the foundation that sustains us in difficult times, and the refuge of love and joy on happy days. Through our families, we learn the values that shape us and receive unconditional support through every stage of life. No family is perfect because we ourselves are not perfect.

Genesis 1:27-28:

God created man and woman and blessed them, commanding them to be fruitful and multiply, thus establishing the basis of the family.

Feelings and Spirits.

Whenever you feel any kind of emotion such as envy, fear, insecurity, hatred, dread, or depression, pray to God to free you from these feelings, because they do not come from Him. He can do all things. It is simple: just talk to Him and ask Him to purify your mind, heart, and soul, renewing you daily. Your mind will be cleansed and purified. Believe in Him.

We are not perfect, and sometimes we struggle with feelings that enslave us. We need to ask God to help us and set us free from all of them—and He will. These are the words of Jesus:

John 15:7-11 (ARA)

If you abide in me and my words abide in you, you will ask whatever you wish, and it will be done for you. In this, my Father is glorified, that you bear much fruit and so become my disciples. As the Father has loved me, so have I loved you; abide in my love. If you keep my commandments, you will abide in my love, just as I have kept my Father's commandments and abide in His love. I have told you these things so that my joy may be in you, and that your joy may be complete.

God is wonderful and renews us every morning. If we ask Him, He cleanses us and fills us with hope and love.

Pray that God will open your spiritual eyes so you can read the Bible and understand, so that you can be born again. Spiritual blindness is the inability to understand the truth.

You will also begin to notice how many people do not see or understand God, but know this: it is because they are still spiritually blind, just as you once were. For them, only the visible world is real. The world is the center of everything for them, but not for us. We are only passing through; this world is not our home.

Spiritual understanding allows us to see beyond what human eyes can see and to realize that, regardless of the circumstances we face, a good and blessed future is ahead. This understanding grows as we know God's Word and walk by faith.

Israel, the Center of All Things.

Did you know that Israel is part of God's love story and that it is the center of all things—where everything began and where everything will end with Jesus' return? Jesus warned us to pay attention to Israel because it will always be the center of all things, of all events, from the beginning of the world until the final day.

Jesus will return to Jerusalem, to the Mount of Olives, where He ascended to heaven after His resurrection. His return will include the restoration of Israel and the establishment of a Messianic Kingdom—a future period when the Messiah will reign and bring peace and love to the world.

The enemy seeks to destroy Israel, using powerful people and leaders, because he understands that this nation is central to God's plan of redemption. The birth, death, resurrection, and eventual return of Jesus are all linked to Israel. That is why the enemy actively opposes God's plan, trying to destroy Israel and prevent the fulfillment of God's promises.

Daniel's prophecy suggests that the 70th week, connected to Israel, will witness the completion of God's plan and the fulfillment of the promises made to David and Abraham.

Details: Israel and Brazil

	Israel	**Brazil**
Inhabitants	9,757,000	216,422,000
Region	Near East	South America
Area	22,070 km²	8,515,770 km²

Your Soul Will Live Forever

Look how small Israel is, and yet no one can destroy it. All the surrounding nations desire to destroy it. However, Israel remains under God's divine protection. No one will ever be able to destroy it. It is amazing!

God chose Israel as His people for several reasons:

- To fulfill the promise of bringing the Messiah and Savior, Jesus Christ – already fulfilled.
- To teach other nations about God.
- To be a nation of priests, prophets, and missionaries to the world.

God's intention was not only to bring forth the Messiah through Israel but also to make Israel a distinct people, leaders who would guide others to the truth and toward God's redemption. Sadly, Israel failed in this mission. The ultimate purpose, however, was the coming of the Messiah, which was fulfilled by Jesus Christ.

Unfortunately, the majority of Jews today do not accept Jesus as the Son of God. They are still waiting for the Messiah. But one day, God will open their eyes, and everyone will bow before Him. One day, all will recognize that Jesus is the King of Kings—the true Messiah.

Philippians 2:10-11

"That at the name of Jesus every knee should bow, in heaven and on earth and under the earth, and every tongue confess that Jesus Christ is Lord, to the glory of God the Father."

The name *Israel* was given to Jacob, a faithful prophet who lived centuries before Christ. The name means "he who prevails with God" or "may God prevail."

129

According to the Bible, the final attack on the land of Israel is prophesied in Revelation 20. The passage says:

"You will attack my people, Israel, like a storm cloud that comes to cover the earth."

The Bible also assures us that the Lord protects Israel and never sleeps.

Psalm 121:4-6 says:

"The protector of the people of Israel never sleeps or slumbers. The Lord will guard you; He is always by your side to protect you. The sun will not harm you by day, nor the moon by night."

In Numbers 24:9, Scripture describes Israel as a mighty lion and says:

"Whoever blesses the people of Israel will be blessed."

That is why I speak about praying for Israel every day of your life—because God will bless those who bless them.

The return of the Messiah, Jesus, is drawing near. Everything points to it. So many signs are already unfolding, little by little, yet many do not see them because they are preoccupied with personal matters. Others see but still do not care. If they do not understand the spiritual reality, they will be blind to the truth and will be lost when Jesus returns, easily deceived by false prophets and false doctrines.

But true Christians—those who have the Spirit of God and know the Word—will understand everything that is happening.

They are prepared because they read and study the Bible. This is how God speaks to us—through His Word.

Matthew 25:31-41

31   "When the Son of Man comes in His glory with all the angels, He will sit on His throne in heavenly glory...."

God Fills What the World Cannot.

Without God and Jesus in our lives, we will never be truly complete or happy. You know that emptiness you try to fill every day with one thing or another? Nothing will satisfy or complete us unless we give ourselves to Jesus, our Savior. When we do, everything begins to make more sense—even in difficult times. We become more prepared for what is to come because God strengthens us and opens our eyes to things we could not see before. He gives us spiritual understanding and wisdom.

This understanding is available to everyone, but we must desire it and ask God for help. He will never refuse to help you. Because He created us and longs to win our hearts, but He will never force us. We have free will. The choice is ours.

Prayer is more powerful than we often realize. The more you read or listen to God's Word, the more your faith will grow. You will become stronger, more courageous, and you will never want to stop praying. Prayer moves mountains, transforms lives, and saves souls.

And remember—every person, whether we like them or not, is a living soul created by God. Sometimes, they are simply lost souls searching for direction, not knowing where to turn. They need Jesus. It is up to us to help them by sharing God's Word. We are called to plant the seed, and God will take care of the rest. Amen, Lord.

Colossians 1:16-18

"For in Him all things were created: things in heaven and on earth, visible and invisible... all things have been created through Him and for Him. He is before all things, and in Him all things hold together. And He is the head of the body, the church... so that in everything He might have the supremacy."

God Does not See People the Way We See Them. God Sees the Heart.

We are all loved by God in the same infinite way. God does not see people the way we do. He sees what we cannot see— He sees who we truly are, not just what we appear to be on the surface. While we often focus on our weaknesses, God sees our potential. He chooses the rejected, the timid, the forgotten, and makes them courageous and victorious.

We tend to value outward gifts, physical beauty, social status, family background, education, and intellect. But God looks deeper. While we worry about what is external and temporary, the Lord looks at the heart—what is eternal.

Glory be to God, who continues to help us even when we do not realize it and even when we do not deserve it. His love is intense and unending.

Remember how God chose David to reign as king? David was the youngest of Jesse's eight sons. His seven older brothers were strong warriors who served King Saul in battle against the Philistines, while David stayed behind tending sheep, playing the harp, and singing. Yet God chose *him*—a humble shepherd—to be king. He anointed David and prepared him for leadership. David's courage and trust in God led to his rise as a warrior and, eventually, as king of Israel. He reigned for 40 years—7 in Hebron and 33 in Jerusalem—establishing a strong and unified kingdom. He was deeply blessed by the Most High, the God of Abraham.

Above all, David was brave and full of faith. His victory over Goliath is one of the most powerful stories of courage and trust in God. As we read in *1 Samuel 17*, David believed that the battle belonged to the Lord and that the armies of the living God would never be defeated.

1 Samuel 16:7

But the Lord said to Samuel, "Do not consider his appearance or his height, for I have rejected him. The Lord does not see as man sees: man sees the appearance, but the Lord sees the heart."

God is Great, Powerful and Attentive to Detail.

Just as I see God as powerful and majestic, I also see how deeply He cares about the smallest details. I have a strong desire to do what is right to please my Creator, even though I often fall short. How can He still have time for me—a small person in such an infinite world, surrounded by people far greater in influence and importance? How can God and Jesus still care about me and listen when I call on them for help?

It is a wonderful comfort to know that He hears us, and that our God teaches us to walk with Him. Regardless of who we are, all we have to do is call out to Him, and He will give us the wisdom that comes from above.

Sometimes this truth can be difficult to grasp, but we should remember what God said about children: that the kingdom of heaven belongs to them, because they are pure and quick to believe.

God wants us to understand that our salvation comes through the Lord Jesus, who died for each one of us. All our sins—even those we have not yet committed, and even those of people who have not been born yet—have already been forgiven through His sacrifice, giving us the opportunity to receive eternal life and dwell with Him in Paradise.

All we must do is ask for forgiveness and be born again—accept Him publicly, be baptized, change our lives, and follow Him.

God forgives sins when there is true repentance and confession. He is faithful and just to forgive us and cleanse us from all unrighteousness.

Matthew 19:14

Then Jesus said, "Let the children come to me, and do not hinder them, for the kingdom of heaven belongs to those who are like them."

Jesus and the Lost Sheep.

The Parable of the Lost Sheep (Meaning: Each One of Us)

Luke 15:1–7

1   All the publicans and "sinners" were gathering to listen to him.

2   But the Pharisees and the teachers of the law criticized him: "This man receives sinners and eats with them."

3   Then Jesus told them this parable:

4   "Which of you, having a hundred sheep and losing one, does not leave the ninety-nine in the field and go after the lost sheep until he finds it?

5   And when he has found it, he joyfully puts it on his shoulders

6   and goes home. When he arrives, he gathers his friends and neighbors and says, 'Rejoice with me, for I have found my lost sheep.

7   I tell you that, in the same way, there will be more joy in heaven over one sinner who repents than over ninety-nine righteous people who have no need to repent."

- Jesus tells the parable of a shepherd who has a hundred sheep, and one gets lost.
- The shepherd leaves the ninety-nine and goes after the one that is lost.

- When he finds it, he places it on his shoulders and returns home.
- Then he calls his friends and neighbors and says, "Rejoice with me, for I have found my lost sheep."

The meaning of the parable:

- The lost sheep represents the lost human being.
- Jesus is the Good Shepherd, reflecting the image of God who seeks out the lost.

Luke 15:7–10

"I tell you, in the same way, there is more joy in heaven over one sinner who repents than over ninety-nine righteous people who do not need to repent."

Spiritual Problem.

The problem of the human race is a spiritual one: man's spirit is separated from God. He hates, lies, cheats, quarrels, kills, and wages war because his spirit is not at peace with God. Therefore, humanity needs to be reconciled with God. What does a dead man need? He needs life. And Jesus Himself declares that He is the life that spiritually dead people need.

Jesus said, "I am the resurrection and the life. He who believes in me, though he were dead, yet shall he live" (John 11:25).

Today, we are very close to Jesus' return. We no longer have time to delay our decision about following Him. That choice must be made today—now—because tomorrow may be too late. Is it worth living for this passing world and losing everything you have strived for all your life? Will your name and your story simply be forgotten one day?

Each of us has a purpose in this world. Every person has something that can help bring others to Jesus. We can start by planting small seeds in the lives of those we meet—talking about Him, living in a way that reflects Him, sharing leaflets, videos, YouTube messages, and other content on social media. Today, we have many tools we can use wisely and positively.

But it is impossible for us to convince someone to fully surrender to Jesus—that is God's work. We plant the seed, and then someone else may come along to plant another. This begins to awaken a desire in that person to know Jesus. Then God acts. What we cannot do, He will do. That is how it began for many of us. Someone planted a seed in our hearts until it grew and blossomed. That is when we realize: the veil that once blinded us is lifted.

Jesus spoke of the Comforter—the Holy Spirit:

John 16:7–8

"But I tell you the truth, it is better for you that I go. For if I do not go, the Comforter will not come to you; but if I go, I will send Him to you. When He comes, He will convict the world of sin, righteousness, and judgment."

The Holy Spirit produces spiritual fruit in our lives—love, joy, peace, patience, kindness, goodness, faithfulness, gentleness, and self-control.

In John 14:16–17, Jesus said that the Spirit would be the Comforter—the Spirit of Truth—who would remain with us forever.

We are Ready, Lord.

The Bible clearly teaches that Jesus will return, but the exact time of His second coming remains unknown. As stated in Matthew 24:36:

But about that day or hour no one knows, not even the angels in heaven, nor the Son, but only the Father.

Although the timing is a mystery, Scripture urges believers to stay prepared and alert. Matthew 24:42 reinforces this with the command:

Therefore keep watch, because you do not know on what day your Lord will come.

Many people who know Jesus and have given their lives to Him often wonder and ask, "When will Jesus come back?" We are ready, Lord. Sometimes we long to be with Him, not wanting to waste more time in a world that is growing more chaotic by the day.

Many are counting down the days until Jesus' return because life in this temporary world is hard—it is filled with trials and suffering. So many are weary and cry out to Jesus, asking Him to come back so we can finally be with Him. We know that once we are with Him, it will be forever.

The things of this world are only enjoyed temporarily—material blessings we receive through hard work, but they do not last. Love between people seems to have faded, and respect is becoming rare. It is heartbreaking to witness what this new generation of children is being taught in public schools—teachings that often contradict the Bible.

If possible, some parents send their children to private Christian schools, where Jesus remains the center. But what about the many who do not have that option and must send their children to public schools, where moral values are being stripped away?

We must pray that the Lord has mercy on this generation, because these children will become the leaders of tomorrow.

Today, many children are confused—even about who they are. It is heartbreaking. The more unusual they are, the more society embraces them. "The stranger, the better"—that is the new saying.

But remember: it all starts at home. We must talk to our children about God, pray for them, and take them to church. We should encourage them to read the Word of the Lord from a young age so that it takes root in their hearts. When the seed is planted early, the world will not be able to deceive them as easily. And even if they stray from the Lord, they are likely to return—because nothing in this world can satisfy like the spiritual nourishment that God's Word provides.

Only God can save, but He can use us to help lead our loved ones to Him.

We must guide our children toward Jesus, planting the seed—and God will make it grow.

He will do what we cannot.

He is the God of the impossible.

Everything in this world is temporary and hollow—an illusion that slowly consumes us.

Sometimes life presents us with difficult and confusing situations, and we do not understand why. But no matter how hard things get, we must never give up on God. He is the Creator, the owner of all things, and He is always in control—even when we do not understand His ways.

Isaiah 26:4

Trust in the Lord forever, for the Lord, the Lord alone is the eternal Rock.

Psalm 125:1

Those who trust in the Lord are like Mount Zion, which cannot be moved but stands forever.

Hebrews 13:14

For this world is not our permanent home; we are looking forward to a home that is yet to come.

Jesus' Promise to Each of Us.

John 14:2–3

In my Father's house are many dwellings; if it were not so, I would have told you. I will prepare a place for you. And if I go and prepare a place for you, I will come again and receive you to myself, so that where I am, you may be also.

This is Jesus' promise to all who accept Him as their Savior. The Bible is the only book in the world that speaks of the past, the present, and the future. It is the ultimate source of truth, and God is faithful to keep His promises.

The Bible reveals God's promises for our lives. Declare them over yourselves and your families! Freedom from addictions, deliverance from sin and evil, financial provision, hope for lost and hurting family and friends, victory over depression, restored marriages, good health, healing, freedom from fear and anxiety, strength, and so much more—these are the blessings God promises to those who believe in Him.

Jesus promised His followers many things, including eternal life, forgiveness, and the Holy Spirit. He also promised that He would always be with us.

Matthew 28:20

"...teaching them to obey everything I have commanded you. And I will be with you always, to the very end of the age."

Jesus sought out the lost.

145

He came to seek and save those who were far from Him—even when they could not come to Him on their own. Jesus was chosen to be the Savior, and through Him, people can be healed.

He loved us when we could not love Him.

He gave us life when we could not find it ourselves.

He sought us out when we were completely lost.

Jeremiah 29:13

You will seek me and find me when you search for me with all your heart.

Before you finish this book, take this opportunity to give yourself into God's hands and accept Jesus. Do not close this page without choosing Him.

Maybe this is the last chance God is giving you to save your soul—we do not know.

John 3:16

For God so loved the world that He gave His one and only Son, that whoever believes in Him shall not perish but have eternal life.

Do not Let Anger Control the Situation— You Serve a Living God Who Can Change Everything

Have you ever been in a situation where someone seemed to have total control over your emotions? How can a single word, a careless action, or an unfair judgment spark such intense emotion within you?

Understand this: anger is not something others cause in you—it is something you allow to rise within yourself. As I have mentioned before, anger is a spirit.

If you learn to change the way you think, respond, and carry yourself, you can become immune to people who try to steal your peace.

Many believe that anger is simply a reaction to external events, but in reality, it is deeper than that—it is spiritual. The same words or actions that make one person laugh can make another furious. That is because the reaction does not come from outside—it comes from within.

People do not make you angry; you choose how to feel and how to act. When you understand how to fight the invisible battles—those spiritual conflicts—you begin to act with wisdom and discernment, not emotion.

They understand that the most intelligent person in the room is not the one who shouts the loudest, but the one who stays calm and composed, who thinks before speaking, and when they do speak, they speak with wisdom and authority.

Why do certain words shake you? It comes down to one thing: we allow them to.

But here is the truth—you serve a living God who gives you strength, identity, and peace. When you stand firm in who you are in Christ, no word spoken against you can break you. People's opinions may come and go, but God's truth about you never changes.

You do not have to give others that kind of power. Let God's voice be the loudest in your life. People do not create your anger; you have the choice to either fall into it or respond wisely. Do not allow anger to dictate your actions. Instead, view this as an opportunity to grow stronger, with God's guidance.

Your emotions are not controlled by others unless you allow them to be. No one can rule your heart unless you grant them that power. But when God is in control, His peace calms every storm.

You always have a choice: to respond in anger or to stay calm and continue your day in peace. God empowers you with the strength to choose wisely.

Taking time to think before acting is a mark of wisdom and maturity. Acting impulsively, without considering the consequences, often leads to regret, embarrassment, or unnecessary pain. But when you pause, reflect, and invite God into your reactions, He empowers you to act with grace, self-control, and purpose.

1 Thessalonians 1:9

For they themselves declare from us what manner of entrance we had to you, and how you turned to God from idols to serve the living and true God.

Deuteronomy 5:26

"For who is there of all flesh who has heard the voice of the living God speaking out of the midst of the fire, as we have, and has lived?".

Joshua 3:10

Then you will know that the living God is among you and that He will surely drive out before you the Canaanites, Hittites, Hivites, Pherezeans, Girgashites, Amorites, and Jebusites.

Is Your Name in the Book of Life?

What is the Book of Life?

The Book of Life is a crucial part of the final judgment. It contains the names of all those who will be saved. It represents the promise of eternal security for the elect.

In the Bible, the Book of Life is the record of those who have trusted in Jesus Christ as their Savior and who will live forever in Heaven. It is also called the Lamb's Book of Life—a list of names belonging to those redeemed by Christ.

Revelation 3:5

The overcomer will also be clothed in white. I will never erase his name from the Book of Life, but I will acknowledge him before my Father and His angels.

Revelation 21:27

Nothing impure will ever enter it, nor will anyone who does what is shameful or deceitful, but only those whose names are written in the Lamb's Book of Life.

In contrast, those who reject God's Word—people who have not placed their faith in Jesus Christ, and those who follow false teachers—do not have their names written in the Book of Life.

Revelation 20:11–15

11   And I saw a great white throne and Him who sat on it, from whose presence the earth and the heaven fled away, and no place was found for them.

12   And the dead, small and great, stood before God, and the books were opened; and another book was opened, which is the Book of Life. And the dead were judged out of those things which were written in the books, according to their works.

13   And the sea gave up the dead which were in it, and death and hell gave up the dead which were in them, and they were judged every man according to their works.

14   And death and hell were cast into the lake of fire. This is the second death.

15   And he who was not found written in the book of life was cast into the lake of fire.

How Can You Be Sure That Your Name Is Written in The Book Of Life?

John 3:3

"Truly, I say to you, no one can see the kingdom of God unless he is born again"

(John 3:5)

"Truly, truly, I say to you, unless one is born of water and the Spirit, he cannot enter the kingdom of God"

John 3:5

That which is born of the flesh is flesh; and that which is born of the Spirit is spirit"

Being written in the Book of Life means being saved and receiving eternal life. It guarantees life on Judgment Day. It also means being enrolled in the true Church of Christ.

Being erased from the Book of Life means dying without the presence of Jesus and God—forever.

According to the Bible, your name is written in the Book of Life when you:

- Believe that Jesus is the Son of God, who died to give us eternal life.
- Ask forgiveness for your sins in Jesus' name.
- Publicly accept Jesus Christ as your Savior (through baptism).
- Are born again and live a changed life after baptism.
- Follow His teachings.
- Acknowledge Jesus as your Lord and Savior.

Have faith that God sent His only Son so that all who believe in Him may have eternal life. Believe that Jesus is the Son of God who died for the sins of the world. Jesus was saying that spiritual birth is a prerequisite for entering the Kingdom of God. This spiritual birth is different from physical birth, because only the Holy Spirit can give birth to spiritual life.

Prayer of Surrender To The Lord.

If you want to surrender your life to God but do not know how to begin, pray like this:

"Lord Jesus, I confess my sins and ask for Your forgiveness. Come into my heart as my Lord and Savior. Take full control of my life and help me to follow in Your footsteps every day, by the power of the Holy Spirit. Thank You, Lord, for saving me and for answering my prayer. Amen."

It is not enough to simply believe in Jesus. Many people know Him and believe in Him, yet still end up lost after death. Even Satan believes in Jesus and fears Him.

There is a big difference between believing, accepting, surrendering, and serving Him.

Romans 10:13 (NIV) – "…for "whoever calls on the name of the Lord will be saved.'"

God will do incredible things in your life—things beyond what you can imagine. He does what we cannot do.

Amen.

1 Thessalonians 5:17 – *Pray without ceasing.*

I pray, in the name of our Lord Jesus Christ, that everyone who reads this book will be richly blessed. May God, in His infinite mercy, lead you to eternal life in His glorious presence.

Take this sacred moment to open your heart and receive Jesus as your Lord and Savior. When you do, your name will be written in the Lamb's Book of Life—the book of eternal hope and redemption.

I pray that you will make eternal life with Jesus your highest priority, and that you will not simply exist, but truly live—guided by God's purpose, filled with His joy, and covered by His grace.

May your life become a shining light, through which God reaches and saves many more souls for His Kingdom. May you live a full, meaningful, and victorious life in the name of Jesus.

All glory to our King, Jesus Christ!

Amen.

www.ingramcontent.com/pod-product-compliance
Lightning Source LLC
Chambersburg PA
CBHW071750120626
46550CB00002B/734